# Schopenhauer

## His Life and Scholarly Activity

# Schopenhauer

## His Life and Scholarly Activity

Written by

Ernest Karlovich Watson

Translated by

Filip Poutintsev

Original Russian edition published in 1891:
Биографическая библиотека Флорентия Павленкова:
Артур Шопенгауэр. Его жизнь и научная деятельность
Эрнест Карлович Ватсон

ISBN: 9798249720834

Publisher: Filip Poutintsev
poutintsev.com
filip@poutintsev.com

Translation: Filip Poutintsev

Copyright © 2026 Filip Poutintsev. All rights reserved.

Cover Photograph: Arthur Schopenhauer, 1859
Cover design: Filip Poutintsev

# Table of Contents

Translator's Foreword..........................................6

Introduction........................................................9

Chapter: I..........................................................13

Chapter: II.........................................................30

Chapter: III........................................................41

Chapter: IV........................................................57

Chapter: V.........................................................77

Chapter: VI........................................................90

Chapter: VII......................................................108

Sources.............................................................121

# Translator's Foreword

This volume presents an English translation of a biographical and philosophical study of Arthur Schopenhauer written by Ernest Karlovich Watson, which was published in the encyclopedic book series: *Biographical Library of Florenty Pavlenkov.*

Ernest Karlovich Watson (1839–1891) was born in Volokolamsk (Moscow region), where his father, a descendant of a Scottish emigrant, served as a district physician. In 1860, Watson graduated from Moscow University in the Faculty of History and Philology.

Watson was not a professional philosopher in the academic sense, nor did he aspire to construct an original philosophical system. His strength lay elsewhere. He was a careful reader, an able synthesizer, and a gifted expositor. Watson belongs to the generation of late nineteenth-century Russian authors whose task was not merely to inform, but to mediate European intellectual life for the educated Russian reader. His works stand at the intersection of biography, history of ideas, and philosophical exposition.

In his portraits of thinkers, he sought to unite three elements: the external facts of a life, the internal logic of a doctrine, and the psychological character of the person behind the ideas. This approach is especially evident in the present work on Arthur Schopenhauer, where Watson consistently moves between biography, philosophy, and cultural context without isolating one from the others.

The intellectual environment in which Watson worked should be kept in mind. Russian philosophy of the late nineteenth century was deeply engaged with German thought, and Schopenhauer occupied a special position in this reception. He was read not only as a philosopher, but as a moral psychologist, a critic of modern optimism, and a stylist of exceptional clarity. Watson's study reflects this multifaceted interest. It does not reduce Schopenhauer to a single formula, nor does it treat his pessimism as a mere personal disposition. Instead, it presents it as a coherent worldview, rooted in metaphysics, ethics, and psychology.

As a writer, Watson combines a sober documentary tone with a clear didactic intention. He quotes extensively from letters and contemporary testimonies, yet he also allows himself evaluative remarks and interpretive syntheses. His language is shaped by the conventions of serious nonfiction of his time, aiming at precision, balance, and accessibility rather than rhetorical flourish. This makes his work particularly valuable as a historical document of Schopenhauer's early reception in Russia.

In this translation, care has been taken to preserve the character of Watson's prose and the structure of his argument, while rendering it into clear and natural English. The aim has been fidelity to meaning rather than mechanical literalism, especially where Russian syntactic patterns would sound unnatural or misleading in English. Philosophical terminology has been kept consistent, with attention to established English usage in Schopenhauer scholarship.

Watson's work should be read not as a modern critical biography, but as a thoughtful and informed nineteenth-century interpretation of Schopenhauer as a man and as a thinker. Its value lies precisely in this perspective. It allows the contemporary reader to see Schopenhauer not only through the lens of later academic debates, but as he appeared to an intelligent and philosophically literate observer of his own era.

This translation is offered in the hope that Ernest Karlovich Watson will be recognized not merely as a compiler or popularizer, but as a serious interpreter of philosophical culture, whose work still repays careful reading today.

# Introduction

Arthur Schopenhauer, one of the most original and remarkable thinkers of the nineteenth century, became known and famous, strictly speaking, only after his death. During his lifetime, professional scholars and philosophers deliberately ignored him, while the general public, by the very nature and character of Schopenhauer's activity, could not take any particular interest in his works. Only a few years after his death, from the end of the 1860s, did interest in his writings and in his teaching begin to manifest itself not only in his homeland, Germany, but also in France and in our own country, Russia. We consider it not superfluous to quote here an interesting excerpt from a letter by L. N. Tolstoy to A. A. Fet, dated August 30, 1869, which appeared in print only a few months ago (published in *Russkoe obozrenie*, May 1890, in the article "V. P. Botkin, I. S. Turgenev, and Count L. N. Tolstoy. From the Memoirs of A. A. Fet"). This is what L. N. Tolstoy wrote:

"Do you know what this summer has truly been for me? An unceasing rapture over Schopenhauer and a series of spiritual delights such as I have never experienced. I ordered all his works and read them, and am reading them (I have also read Kant). And surely no student during his course of study ever learned so much and came to know so much as I have this summer. I do not know whether I shall ever change my opinion, but now I am convinced that Schopenhauer is the most genial of men. You say that he is so-so, that he wrote something or other on philosophical subjects. Something or other? It is the whole world reflected with incredible clarity and beauty. I have begun translating him. Will you not also undertake a translation of him? We could publish it together. Reading him, it is incomprehensible to me how his name can remain unknown. There is only one explanation, the very one he so often repeats, that 'apart from idiots, there is almost no one in the world...'"

On February 14, 1888, the Moscow Psychological Society solemnly commemorated, at a ceremonial meeting in the assembly hall of Moscow University, the centenary of the birth of "one of the greatest German thinkers of the present century, Arthur Schopenhauer." On that occasion, the deputy chairman of the Society, Professor N. A. Zverev, presented the most essential facts of Schopenhauer's life, and three other speakers, members of the Society, delivered addresses on the significance of his philosophy. Subsequently, these speeches were published together in a single volume, supplemented by a more detailed biographical sketch of Schopenhauer compiled by a member of the said Society, V. I. Shtein.

With the widespread, at the end of the 1870s, pessimistic philosophy both in Western Europe and in our country, a closer acquaintance with Schopenhauer and his teaching also began. In 1881 Schopenhauer's principal work, *The World as Will and Representation*, was translated into Russian. In 1886 his works *On the Fourfold Root of the Principle of Sufficient Reason* and *On the Will in Nature* were likewise translated (both translations belong to A. A. Fet, who thus fulfilled the advice given to him back in 1869 by Count L. N. Tolstoy; to the first of these translations a preface by N. N. Strakhov was appended). Schopenhauer's *Aphorisms and Maxims* and *The Fundamental Problems of Ethics* were also translated, works which, owing to their relative popularity, achieved wider circulation in society.

Until very recently, very little was known about Schopenhauer's life. All his biographers unanimously acknowledge that it is extremely difficult, almost impossible, to write a reasonably detailed biography of him, first, because, like, for example, Descartes, he led a very secluded and solitary life, and second, because until recently there were almost no suitable sources for his biography. Schopenhauer himself regarded with extreme lack of sympathy the efforts of biographers to collect in advance materials for future biographies of people notable in one respect or another, and he felt a positive antipathy toward autobiographies. The autobiographical note he sent at the request of the editors of Meyer's *Conversations-Lexicon*, printed in the first issue of the *Proceedings of the Moscow Psychological Society* and dated May 28, 1851, occupies literally no more than sixty-four lines of large type.

# Chapter: I

**Schopenhauer's ancestors – His parents – Characterization of Schopenhauer's father and mother – Schopenhauer's childhood years – His recollections – His numerous journeys in childhood and adolescence – Schopenhauer does not wish to become a merchant – The death of Schopenhauer's father**

For the most part, it happens that interest in the parents and forebears of people who have become famous in some field of human activity arises only when the lives of those forebears have already mainly become shrouded in the midst of the past. This, however, cannot be said of Schopenhauer's ancestors and parents.

On his father's side, Arthur Schopenhauer was descended from a fairly distinguished Danzig family. Even his great-grandfather, Andreas Schopenhauer, had the honor, as one of the wealthiest and most respected citizens of Danzig, of receiving Peter the Great and his wife Catherine in his home during their travels through Germany. The son of Andreas Schopenhauer, Arthur's grandfather, Johann Friedrich Schopenhauer, considerably increased the family's wealth; for the most part, he lived not in Danzig itself but near the city, on his villa close to the village of Ora. Arthur's grandmother, Renata, née Sermans, also belonged to a distinguished family; after her husband's death, a guardianship was established over her and over her elder son, Andreas Michael Schopenhauer, since both showed signs of mental disorder. Her younger son, Heinrich Floris Schopenhauer, Arthur's father, traveled widely in his youth and later inherited the greater part of his father's and grandfather's fortune, maintaining with honor the reputation of his family.

Heinrich Floris Schopenhauer was a man of medium height, solidly built, broad-faced, like his son, who later became famous. Despite belonging by birth to the local patriciate and aristocracy, Arthur's father was imbued with ideas of justice and freedom, which earned him the affection and esteem of his fellow citizens. Fearlessness, straightforwardness, and candor were the distinguishing traits of his character; at the same time, he was extremely hot-tempered and stubborn. One of Arthur Schopenhauer's biographers relates the following episode, which vividly characterizes his father's decisiveness and rectilinearity and won him still greater respect and sympathy among his fellow citizens. Danzig, as is well known, until the end of the eighteenth century was one of the Hanseatic republics, surrounded on all sides by Polish territories. When, after the first partition of Poland, Frederick the Great conceived the plan of annexing this city as well, together with the part of what is now West Prussia that had fallen to his dominion, to the Kingdom of Prussia, the citizens of the old Hanseatic republic refused to recognize Prussian rule. It resolved not to admit the Prussians into the city. As a result, Prussian troops blockaded Danzig by land and cut off the supply of foodstuffs. The commander of the besieging corps took up residence at Schopenhauer's villa. As a reward for the hospitality shown him there, though enforced, he ordered that the owner be offered a pass for bringing fodder into the city for Heinrich Floris Schopenhauer's horses. Schopenhauer, however, instructed that the general be thanked and informed that he still had sufficient fodder for the time being, and that when it was exhausted, he would have his horses slaughtered. This ardent love for the independence of his native city, Floris, was expressed not only in words but in deeds. He declined an offer made to him by the Prussian king to settle in Prussia. When, in 1793, the annexation of Danzig to Prussia was definitively decided, he liquidated all his affairs in Danzig within twenty-four hours, something that could not be accomplished without substantial losses, and moved to the Hanseatic Republic of Hamburg.

Heinrich Floris Schopenhauer was not only a fervent patriot and an able businessman but also a man of broad education. During his frequent business trips to England and France, he managed to acquire a fairly thorough acquaintance with the literature of those countries; his favorite author was Voltaire. The political and family order of England pleased him so much that for a time, he even considered settling there permanently. Although this plan did not come to fruition, he arranged his household entirely in the English manner and not only read the *Times* from cover to cover every day himself but also made his son read this newspaper from the earliest years.

At the age of thirty-eight, Heinrich Floris Schopenhauer married eighteen-year-old Anna Henriette Trosiener, the daughter of a respected though not wealthy Danzig councilman. She was a petite, graceful, blue-eyed, fair-haired young woman. Her education was rather superficial, like that of all young women of the time, not only of the middle but even of the upper classes; yet her natural intelligence and wit partly compensated for the lack of education. She never became a devoted housekeeper. She herself frankly admitted that she felt no passionate love for her fiancé, who at that time was more than twice her age, nor did he lay claim to such love. She openly said that she married Heinrich Floris Schopenhauer in the expectation of a more brilliant environment and life than she found in her parental home. Schopenhauer's biographers emphasize the fact that the author of *The World as Will and Representation* owed his origin not to a marriage of love. The insufficient education she had received in her parents' home, she partly supplemented later during many years of life with her intelligent and educated husband. In this respect, great assistance was provided by her husband's excellent library, rich in the best English and French books of the time. In this intensive reading, she found a capable guide in the person of her childhood friend, the Anglican pastor in Danzig, Jamieson. Immediately after the wedding, she undertook a long journey with her husband, who had an inborn passion for travel. They went through Berlin, Hanover, and Pyrmont to Frankfurt am Main, which, in her words, strongly reminded her of her wealthy and free native city of Danzig, and from there, through Belgium and Paris, to England. There, at Heinrich Floris's wish, they intended to remain longer, so that their firstborn, whose birth they were expecting, might be born precisely in his beloved England and thus, as it were, acquire by birth the rights of English citizenship. Circumstances, however, forced them to abandon this plan, and after an arduous journey, they arrived in Danzig, where a few days later, on February 22, 1788, their eldest son was born. At his baptism on March 3 of the same year, he was given the name Arthur. Heinrich Schopenhauer chose this name because it has no specifically German coloring and is pronounced almost exactly the same in other languages, French and English.

Arthur Schopenhauer's father, a native and citizen of the free Hanseatic city of Danzig, as we have seen above, always distinguished himself by love of freedom and sympathy for France. The Great French Revolution, which broke out a little more than a year after the birth of the future famous philosopher, further strengthened these inclinations and sympathies. When Arthur was five years old, in 1793, the free city of Danzig was again subjected to blockade by royal Prussian troops, and local patriots lost all hope of preserving their republican order. Then Heinrich Floris Schopenhauer resolved to leave his native city altogether. In March of that year, a few hours before the Prussians entered Danzig, the parents departed with their entire family and set out through Swedish Pomerania, which at that time belonged to Sweden, to the free city of Hamburg. There, the doors of the best houses were opened to the educated and prosperous couple; their acquaintance with Klopstock, Field Marshal Kalkreuth, Nelson, Lady Hamilton, and others dates from this period. However, after leaving their native city, the Schopenhauers' passion for travel seems to have grown even stronger. During their twelve-year stay in Hamburg, they undertook a whole series of journeys, more or less distant. One of the purposes of these frequent travels was also the wish of Schopenhauer's father to promote Arthur's all-round development, and later the philosopher recalled this with gratitude, not without reason, comparing his own multifaceted development, due in part to these journeys, with the one-sided development of most German scholars.

At the age of nine, he accompanied his father to France, where his father left him for two years with a good acquaintance, the Le Havre merchant Grégoire, whose son studied together with young Arthur under the best teachers of that city. There he spent the happiest period of his childhood and became completely Gallicized, precisely as his father wished, who wholeheartedly hated German philistinism. When Arthur returned entirely alone by sea from Le Havre to Hamburg, it turned out that he had almost completely forgotten how to speak German, and it took him some effort to become accustomed again to his native speech. At the age of eleven, he entered the private gymnasium of a certain Runge, attended by the sons of the most distinguished citizens. However, since the curriculum of this institution dealt primarily with commercial subjects, and the majority of pupils were children of merchants, Schopenhauer's initial education proved rather one-sided. Thus, for example, Latin, which Arthur had begun studying already in Le Havre, he learned thoroughly, according to his own words, only at the age of nineteen, and then within half a year.

We have already said above that Schopenhauer's father wished to make a merchant of him. However, to the great sorrow of the representative of the old Danzig trading firm, Arthur showed not the slightest inclination toward this. In him, an ardent love for abstract science manifested itself early. For a long time, Heinrich Floris resisted his son's requests. In order to divert Arthur from the idea of entering a gymnasium, he proposed that he accompany him on a new journey undertaken together with his wife in the spring of 1803 to Belgium, England, France, Switzerland, and southern Germany. Later, Schopenhauer himself expressed deep regret that so much precious time for school education had been almost wasted on interesting but still incapable of providing a solid education, wanderings around the world. Nevertheless, with characteristic energy, he did not fail to make up for the lost time through intensive work.

In England, they remained about half a year. In order not to interrupt his son's schooling altogether, the parents, setting out to travel in northern England and Scotland, placed him in the house of a pastor in Wimbledon near London. There, he laid the foundation for a solid acquaintance with the language of a people who, alongside the French, were especially congenial to him.

In this school, alongside general subjects, serious attention was also given to the fine arts: flute playing, singing, drawing, horseback riding, fencing, and dancing. However, the lively and pampered youth, for the first time separated from his family, with no close person near him and left to himself, complained in letters to his parents of the lack of amusements. His mother replied: "Drawing, books, music, fencing, and riding constitute sufficient amusement. More boisterous entertainments do not really befit your age. In order to enjoy those, one must first learn how to live; you are only preparing yourself for that." In another letter, she advised him to occupy himself less with Schiller's tragedies and dramas and to read more in English. "I wish," she wrote, "that you would set aside all poets in general and each of them in particular for the time being and turn to more serious reading. You are only fifteen years old, you have already read and studied the best German, French, and English poets, and yet, apart from the books with which you were obliged to be acquainted during school hours to satisfy Mr. Runge's requirements, and apart from a few novels, you are completely unfamiliar with prose works, with history, for example. A sense of the beautiful in this world as it is cannot serve us as a guiding thread, and I would like to see you become anything at all, only not a so-called *bel esprit* [wit (Fr.)]." On the other hand, Arthur's father, partly agreeing that life in Wimbledon could hardly have seemed especially pleasant to his son, and allowing him to go to London every week for diversion, lamented the poor handwriting of his son and persistently urged him to try to improve it. Such advice was obviously given in view of the old merchant's desire someday to see his son seriously devoted to commercial pursuits.

Schopenhauer, who at that time was only fifteen years old, rebelled in the most resolute and even sharp manner against English cant, which, as he wrote to his mother, "forces him on holidays and Sundays to loiter about doing nothing and instills the wish that truth might at last illuminate with its torch the Egyptian darkness reigning in England." His mother rather spitefully reminded him in reply that earlier she "had had to struggle with him when on Sundays and holidays Arthur did not want to take up anything useful, citing the fact that these were days of rest; now, however, he has suddenly become sated with festive rest." In general, a seriousness beyond his years manifests itself in the youth, or rather in the adolescent. Thus, for example, he writes to his parents that "a visit to Westminster Abbey gave him infinite material for reflection." "Seeing in these Gothic walls the remains and tombs of poets, heroes, and kings as they have been gathered together by passing times, one asks whether they are indeed in communion there, where neither caste boundaries nor notions of time and place divide them, and asks what exactly and how much each has retained in the other world of the splendor and greatness allotted to them on earth. Kings have left their crowns and scepters, poets their fame; but those among them who were truly great in mind, who shone with inner gifts, have preserved in the other world everything that they enjoyed here."

From England, the Schopenhauers traveled through Holland and Belgium to Paris, where they remained for more than two months. There, making use of their connections, they had the opportunity to become acquainted with many of the outstanding figures of France at that time, beginning with the First Consul, Napoleon Bonaparte, and to study all the sights of Paris. The acting of the famous Talma made little impression on the young Schopenhauer, but he greatly enjoyed the short comedies and comic opera. "The French language and French actors," he wrote, "seem to have been created expressly for this kind of play; but to the declamation of French tragedians, cruel and unnatural, I shall hardly ever become accustomed." Schopenhauer later also regarded French verse and declamation with disapproval, but he always praised French prose style, in contrast to the German pomposity of expression. As for the French themselves, whom Schopenhauer, from childhood onward, had many occasions to observe, he acknowledged them as a lively and cheerful people, but sensual and the most frivolous of all European nations. Because of this temperament, they could not be especially congenial to Schopenhauer's serious mind. Indeed, in his writings, one often encounters rather sharp remarks about the French. Thus, for example, in his *Parerga*, he says: "Other parts of the world have produced monkeys; Europe has produced the French. One is worth the other." He further reproaches the French for excessive concern about the opinions of others, allegedly fostering absurd ambition, ridiculous national vanity, and repugnant boasting. As a result, French aspirations themselves acquire such instability that they become the subject of witticisms and mockery for other nations.

At the beginning of January 1804, the Schopenhauer family set out through Orléans, Tours, Angoulême, Bordeaux, and southern France to Hyères. The ruins of the Roman amphitheater in Nîmes made a powerful impression on the young Schopenhauer, bordering on reverence. In Toulon, he was beside himself over the fate of the convicts confined there. In Lyon, he recalls the multitude of people who perished in that city on the scaffold during the Reign of Terror and marvels that "the Lyonnais now stroll as if nothing had happened over the very places where ten years ago their friends and relatives were lined up and shot with grapeshot." "Is it possible," he exclaims, "that their imagination does not depict the bloody spectacle of relatives perishing in torment? Can one believe that present-day Lyonnais, passing through the square, calmly relate how here, on this very spot, their friends were executed? Truly, it is incomprehensible how the power of time dulls vivid and terrible impressions."

From France, the Schopenhauers went to Switzerland. The sight of the Swiss Alps made a powerful impression on Arthur, and he begged his father to allow him to remain longer in Chamonix; even in old age, he became agitated when he needed to speak of Mont Blanc. Among other things, he compares the gloomy mood of highly gifted minds with Mont Blanc, whose summit is usually shrouded in clouds; but "when at times, especially early in the morning, the cloudy veil is torn apart and the mountain's peak, tinged with the purple of sunrise, appears through the clouds at Chamonix, then every heart rejoices. So too in genius, mostly melancholic, a peculiar cheerfulness, arising from complete objectivity of mind and possible only for genius, casts a radiance upon its lofty brow." However, if Schopenhauer delighted in Swiss nature, the Swiss themselves greatly displeased him, and this dislike, born already in adolescence, remained with him throughout his life.

Through Swabia and Bavaria, the Schopenhauers proceeded to Austria, where they were detained at the border for a whole week owing to some irregularity in their passport. This travel adventure is described with great humor by the young Schopenhauer. After seeing Vienna and Pressburg, the travelers went through Moravia, Bohemia, Silesia, and Saxony to Berlin. From there, Schopenhauer's father departed on business to Hamburg, while Arthur and his mother went to Danzig. There, in the autumn of 1804, at the age of sixteen and a half, he was confirmed in the same Church of St. Mary in which he had been baptized in 1788. In December of that year, he returned to Hamburg. Having become well acquainted during his travels in France and England with the French and English languages and having practiced calligraphy at his father's wish, he entered in January 1805, again at his father's express desire, the commercial office of the Hamburg merchant and senator Jenisch.

Only a few months later, in the spring of 1805, Arthur's father died suddenly. He fell from an attic window into a deep canal and drowned. Rumors circulated that Heinrich Floris Schopenhauer, who in the last years of his life had become highly irritable, mainly because of increasing deafness, had deliberately thrown himself into the canal; others asserted that Schopenhauer's father took his own life in a fit of insanity hereditary in his family. Indeed, in several generations of the Schopenhauer family, more than one case of insanity is encountered. Others saw in Heinrich Floris's death merely an accident. Be that as it may, the death of his father produced a strong and oppressive impression on Arthur. Although by nature he was far from all sensitivity and sentimentality, he nevertheless spoke of his father with the greatest warmth in conversation with friends until deep old age.

After Arthur Schopenhauer's death, among his manuscripts was found a dedication written by him already in 1821 but not published at the time, addressed to the memory of his father and intended for the second edition of his famous book *The World as Will and Representation*. This dedication reads:

"A noble, beneficent mind, to whom I owe entirely what I have become. Your provident care protected and cherished me not only throughout my helpless childhood and rash youth, but also in mature age, down to the present day. By giving me life, you, at the same time, took care that your son in this world, as it is, should have all the means to exist and develop, and without this care of yours, I would have hundreds of times stood on the brink of destruction. In my mind, the striving for theoretical investigation of the essence of being predominated too decisively for me, for the sake of securing my own existence, to be able, by doing violence to my intellect, to devote myself to some other activity and set myself the task of earning daily bread. Apparently it was precisely in foreseeing this that you understood that your son was incapable either of plowing the land or of expending his strength on mechanical crafts. Likewise, you, a proud republican, understood that your son lacked the talent either to compete with insignificance and baseness or to cringe before officials, patrons, and their advisers in order basely to beg for a piece of black bread, or finally, by accommodating himself to inflated mediocrity, humbly to join the crowd of scribblers and charlatans praising it. You understood that it was more natural for your son, together with the Voltaire whom you revered, to think: 'Since only two days of life are given to us, it is not worth the trouble to spend them crawling before contemptible knaves.' Therefore, I dedicate my work to you and send you, beyond the grave, the gratitude that I owe to you alone and to no one else. That I was able to develop the powers granted me by nature and to employ them for that for which they were intended; that, following an inborn inclination, I could work unhindered at a time when no one rendered me assistance, for all this I owe to you, my father, to your activity, your intellect, your frugality, and your care for the future. For this, praise to you, my noble father. Let everyone who finds in my work joy, consolation, and instruction hear your name and know that if Heinrich Floris Schopenhauer had not been the man he truly was, then Arthur Schopenhauer would have perished a hundred times over. Thus may my gratitude accomplish the only thing I can accomplish for you, whom you created: may your name be spread as far as my name itself can spread."

# Chapter: II

**Arthur Schopenhauer enters the university – Early manifestations of Schopenhauer's pessimism. Schopenhauer's university years – His literary acquaintances – Cooling of relations between Schopenhauer and his mother**

After her husband's death, Anna Schopenhauer moved with her eight-year-old daughter to Weimar. Mercantile Hamburg was repugnant to her; she was drawn to what was then called the "residence of the Muses." She arrived in that city two days before the Battle of Jena, and a few months later, despite the troubled times, thanks to her sociability, amiability, and talent, she had already managed to become acquainted with and close to almost all the Weimar celebrities of the day. Although her husband's affairs had suffered some disarray in the last period of his life, he nevertheless left the family a fortune substantial enough that his widow could lead a relatively open and expansive social life. In her home, twice a week, people gathered, such as Goethe, Wieland, Grimm, the Schlegel brothers, Prince Pückler, and others. She even gained access to the Weimar court of the time, enjoyed the friendship and favor of Duke Karl August and his consort, the dukes of Saxe-Coburg-Gotha, the hereditary prince of Mecklenburg-Schwerin, and others. A few years later, she herself entered the literary field, and not without success.

Meanwhile, Arthur Schopenhauer, deeply shaken by his father's death, out of respect for his memory, continued for some time longer the commercial career he so detested. To be sure, he did so mainly for appearance's sake. Sitting at his desk with the account books laid out, he secretly read Gall's phrenology or some other similar book, behind his employer's back. However, at last, the hour of deliverance struck for him as well. His mother read one of his letters in which Arthur bitterly complained of his fate to one of his Weimar friends, Fernow. Fernow persuaded his mother not to oppose her son's inclination, not to force him to continue in commerce, and to allow him to enter a university. Schopenhauer, a stranger to all sentimentality, wept for joy upon receiving his mother's letter granting complete freedom to his natural inclinations. On the advice of the same Fernow, he moved to Gotha, where Professor Döring undertook to prepare him in Latin for university entrance, and Professor Jacobs worked with him on German literature. Both spoke in the highest terms of their pupil's remarkable abilities. However, Arthur allowed himself some mockery of certain gymnasium teachers, and when they learned of it, they did not admit him to take the examination for the certificate of maturity. He then decided to move to Weimar and continue preparing for the university there; however, at his mother's request, he did not settle in her house. The motives that led this woman, who sincerely loved her son, to refuse to live with him are interesting. This is what she wrote to Arthur, who at that time was nineteen years old:

"For my happiness, it is necessary to know that you are happy; but we can both be happy even while living apart. I have told you more than once that it is challenging to live with you, and the more closely I look at you, the more obvious this difficulty becomes to me. I will not conceal from you that so long as you remain as you are, I am ready to make any other sacrifice rather than this one. I do not deny your good qualities; what separates me from you is not your inner qualities but your outward manners, your habits, your views, and judgments. In a word, I cannot come to terms with you in anything that concerns the external world. Your perpetual dissatisfaction, your perpetual complaints about what is inevitable, your gloomy appearance, your strange judgments, uttered as though they were oracles, exert upon me a truly oppressive effect.

All this weighs on me but does not convince me in the least. Your endless arguments, your perpetual complaints about the stupidity of the world and the insignificance of man prevent me from sleeping at night and press upon me like a nightmare."

These words of a mother addressed to a nineteen-year-old young man are highly characteristic. They show that the seeds of pessimism, which runs through Schopenhauer's entire life and is felt in almost every line of his later works, revealed themselves in him very clearly and sharply, to the great distress and displeasure of his cheerful mother, already at an age when for other people the world usually still appears in the brightest colors. The nineteen-year-old pessimist settled in Weimar separately from his cheerful, sociable mother.

The young man energetically began striving toward the goal he had set. Lessons with several competent professors and an inborn aptitude for languages enabled him rather quickly to supplement his one-sided and far from systematic early education. Having taken lodgings in the house of the philologist Passow, well known in his time, he made rapid progress under his guidance in acquaintance with the classical languages and classical antiquity. In addition, Arthur studied Latin grammar and Latin syntax with the renowned

Latinist Lenz, director of the Weimar gymnasium, while at the same time filling gaps in his historical and mathematical knowledge. With remarkable zeal, the young man worked not only all day but also at night, and when at twenty-one he entered the then celebrated University of Göttingen, he proved to be as thoroughly and broadly prepared for attending university lectures as few of his fellow students.

At first, he enrolled in the medical faculty. He attended lectures in natural history, but soon, under the influence of G. E. Schulze, he became interested in philosophy and transferred to the philosophy faculty. Schulze had the most decisive and beneficial influence on the future famous philosopher. He advised Arthur first of all to undertake a careful study of Plato and Kant and not to take up either Aristotle or Spinoza until he had become thoroughly acquainted with the two thinkers named above. At least, this is how Schopenhauer himself relates it in autobiographical notes he later drafted. Schopenhauer stayed in Göttingen from 1809 to 1811, and there, among his university companions, he became especially close to the man who later became famous, Bunsen. Naturally unsociable, he took almost no part in the usual noisy student life, and the circle of his acquaintances was limited to very few fellow students, among them the poet

Ernst Schulze, a certain Lücke, and an American named Astor who later became an arch-millionaire. During vacations, Arthur made excursions to the Harz, to Weimar, and to Erfurt, where he happened to be during the famous Congress of Erfurt and was in part an eyewitness to the servility of German ruling princes before Napoleon I. However, this young thinker, already then occupied with the plan of his future major work on "the world as will," apparently was not very interested in that will embodied in a man named Napoleon. Another man interested the future philosopher far more, a genius whose nature was a direct contrast to Napoleon's. In his mother's house, he had already become acquainted with Goethe, who treated the young man with the greatest benevolence. From that time, Schopenhauer began to feel for him, contrary to the basic traits of his own character, an enthusiastic reverence, calling him the most remarkable man of the German people.

In 1811, the twenty-three-year-old Schopenhauer moved from Weimar to Berlin, drawn by the loudly resounding philosophical reputation of Fichte. However, already at that time, the young philosopher had developed too independent a manner of thinking to follow wholly in the footsteps of this thinker, who, in Schopenhauer's opinion, often lapsed into sophistry. He attended

Fichte's lectures very diligently and more than once entered into disputes with him during the colloquia Fichte held; yet soon, as Schopenhauer himself said, his a priori reverence for Fichte gave way to contempt and mockery. Alongside philosophy, he also zealously continued in Berlin the study of the natural sciences: physics, chemistry, astronomy, geognosy, physiology, anatomy, and zoology. Nor did he neglect the classical languages, attending lectures by Wolf, Bekker, Bernhardi, and others. Only jurisprudence and theology did not attract him, and in this respect, a significant gap appeared in his education that made itself felt throughout his later activity. Far more than Fichte's lectures, he was interested in Schleiermacher's lectures on the history of medieval philosophy, though he found them not without a poetic coloring. Finally, he also attended a course on Scandinavian poetry and read the classical writers of the Renaissance, Montaigne, Rabelais, and others.

The troubled times of the period, however, were not especially favorable for peaceful scholarly pursuits. During Schopenhauer's stay in Berlin, the star of Napoleon, which had shone so brightly until then, began to dim, and all Germany, including university circles, was seized by ardent patriotic enthusiasm. However, Schopenhauer, despite being twenty-four years old, was so alien to this enthusiasm that he later even incurred reproaches for lack of patriotism. He was already preparing to take his doctoral examination in Berlin when the uncertain outcome of the battles of Bautzen and Lützen forced him to leave Berlin and seek a more tranquil refuge for his studies in Saxony. During his twelve-day flight to Dresden, he found himself in the very midst of military turmoil. The mayor of a small town, accidentally learning that Schopenhauer spoke French well, made use of his services, and he had to take on the role of interpreter. Arthur spent the summer in the countryside not far from the Saxon town of Rudolstadt, where, amid the surrounding noise of war, he worked out the plan of his treatise *On the Fourfold Root of the Principle of Sufficient Reason*. At the beginning of October, the University of Jena, based on the dissertation Schopenhauer sent, proclaimed him Doctor of Philosophy in absentia. For the winter, he moved to his mother in Weimar.

However, here the difference between the characters of mother and son manifested itself more strongly than ever. Intelligent, educated, and to a certain extent even talented, Anna Schopenhauer could neither understand nor endure the isolation and misanthropy of her son. To this difference in character was added the fact that Schopenhauer, thrifty and calculating from an early age, disapproved of what he considered his mother's overly expansive way of living. He realized, and not without reason, that the activity toward which he felt drawn and to which he considered himself called would hardly be able to provide him with material security, and therefore, he especially valued preserving as intact as possible the family fortune left by his father.

Anna Schopenhauer, being a woman of considerable intelligence, understood that she and her son simply did not match in character. This is what she once wrote to him on the matter:

"I believe you will find it useful for both of us if our mutual relations are arranged so that our independence on both sides suffers no harm and so that I, in particular, preserve the unforced, peaceful, and independent calm that brings comfort into my life. Therefore, Arthur, arrange your existence as though I were not here at all, with the exception that every day from one until three you will come to dine with me. Each evening, we will spend as he pleases, except for two evenings a week when the company gathers at my house. On those evenings you will, of course, come, spend time with the guests, and, if you wish, remain the whole evening and sup with us. On the remaining days of the week, you will take supper and tea at your own home. It will be better so, dear Arthur, for both of us. By this means, we shall preserve our present relationship. Furthermore, your independence will benefit from it. As for diversions, you will have three evenings at your disposal for going to the theater, and two evenings to spend with me. I believe that is enough diversion, though I fear that my evenings will seem less entertaining to you than they do to those guests who, being older and having an advantage over you, play a more prominent role in the evenings. You will be the only quite young man in our society, but the interest of being in the same circle as Goethe will, one must think, compensate you for the merriment you may not find with me. You will be a welcome guest for me, and to make your stay in Weimar more pleasant, I will do everything I can, without sacrificing, of course, my own freedom and peace."

In the opinion of one of Schopenhauer's biographers, Seidlitz, this letter of his mother, like the one quoted above, written in connection with Arthur's intended move to Weimar, fully delineates Arthur Schopenhauer and accurately characterizes him as he was not only in youth but also in maturity. "Out of indulgence, the mother ascribes to an external overlay what is an inalienable feature of her son's inner being, and what probably often manifested itself in her late husband as well, making life with him rather difficult. The young man's habit of pronouncing judgments from on high may be explained by inherited self-confidence. The developed conviction in Arthur Schopenhauer of his own infallibility, his megalomania and gloominess, unquestionably arose based on an inborn abnormality of the nervous system. Of course, one cannot blame the youth for them as something arising from mere willfulness. However, at the same time, one cannot but regret that no one was close enough to Arthur Schopenhauer to exert, through gentleness and exhortation, a firm and beneficial influence on these peculiarities of his mental constitution."

He also did not get along with his sister Adele, who was ten years younger and did not resemble him either in appearance or in character, and thus he remained lonely even within a family setting.

Around this same time, Schopenhauer became acquainted with the actress Jagemann, well known at the time, and became seriously infatuated with her. He later admitted that for a time he was not averse to marrying her, but this plan fell through, and Schopenhauer remained a bachelor for life.

# Chapter: III

**Publication of Schopenhauer's first scholarly works – His journey through Italy – Schopenhauer seeks a university chair – The reception given by criticism to his writings – Schopenhauer as a professor – Schopenhauer leaves the professorship and sets out traveling again – Schopenhauer's lawsuit with Mrs. Marquet – Schopenhauer's life in Dresden – Schopenhauer's second attempt to appear in a professorial chair – Schopenhauer finally renounces academic teaching and settles in Frankfurt am Main**

In 1813, when Schopenhauer was twenty-five, he published at his own expense his first work, on which he had labored diligently first in Berlin and then in Rudolstadt: *On the Fourfold Root of the Principle of Sufficient Reason*. This work immediately attracted attention, elicited favorable notices in periodicals, and drew enthusiastic praise from Schopenhauer's teacher, the Göttingen professor Schulze. Among the majority of the public, however, it passed almost unnoticed, which can be explained in part by the turbulent military and political circumstances Germany was then experiencing. Schopenhauer not only earned nothing from the publication of this book, but he even suffered rather substantial losses. In this connection, it is worth recounting a very characteristic anecdote reported by his biographers. When he presented a copy of his work to his mother, she, having read the title, exclaimed in a jocularly ironic tone: "Ah, so it is about little roots. That must be something in the pharmaceutical line." The son parried his mother's mockery with the remark that his writings would be read, and read intensely, in times when everyone would long since have forgotten the belletristic productions of Mrs. Anna Schopenhauer.

Although Schopenhauer lived in Weimar, not in the same house as his mother, but separately, he disliked her circle and her way of life to such a degree that, after living there about a year, he decided to part from his mother altogether and settle in another city. The young philosopher, unsociable by nature, found that life in Weimar distracted and diverted him too much from the goal he had set himself. On this subject, he wrote as follows about the calling and aims of the philosopher in one of his later letters:

"Philosophy is an Alpine summit, to which only a steep path leads, running over stones and thorns. The higher a man climbs, the more desolate it becomes, and only a man wholly fearless can walk this path. Often, he makes his way above an abyss, and he must have a sound head so as not to succumb to dizziness. However, the world upon which he looks down from above appears to him smooth and level: deserts and swamps vanish, irregularities are smoothed out, and discords do not reach him. He is surrounded by pure air and sunlight, while at his feet lies deep mist."

Thus, in the spring of 1814, Schopenhauer moved from Weimar to Dresden, a city already familiar to him from the journeys he had made in childhood and adolescence with his parents. There, he conceived and wrote his major work, *The World as Will and Representation*.

Despite his characteristic reserve, despite a restraint and sarcasm bordering on conceit, the young philosopher did not live in Dresden as a complete anchorite and, in certain circles, enjoyed exceptional affection and respect. He was especially fond of visiting the famous Dresden Picture Gallery, a thorough acquaintance with which later proved helpful to him in his treatises on art; and, having loved nature passionately since childhood, he traveled much in the surrounding countryside.

Having finished in the autumn of 1818 his work *The World as Will and Representation*, Schopenhauer concluded a contract with the publisher Brockhaus, who paid him one gold ducat per printed sheet; but, not waiting for the publication of the work on which he had labored for four whole years and which made his name famous, he set off traveling in Italy. Possessing a linguistic ability that was relatively rare among Germans, he spoke Italian excellently, which was extremely useful during his stay in Italy. In Rome, where he spent four whole months, and in Naples, most of his acquaintances were Englishmen. There, he partly shook off his unsociability and gave himself over to the enjoyment of art, nature, and Italian life in general. Among Italian poets, Schopenhauer valued Petrarch especially highly, but disliked Dante, finding him overly didactic. He did not rate Ariosto, Boccaccio, Tasso, or Alfieri particularly highly. In the arts, he paid special attention to the sculpture and architecture of the ancient world; he felt less attraction to painting, although, when still a very young man, under the influence of conversations with Goethe, he wrote a very valuable treatise on colors and pigments. He gladly attended the opera in Italy, and Rossini was his favorite composer.

During his stay in Italy, Schopenhauer received a letter from his sister Adele informing him that the Danzig trading house to which his mother had entrusted the greater part of her own and Adele's fortune had gone bankrupt, and that both of them had lost their entire property. Schopenhauer himself, being cautious and suspicious by temperament, had placed only a small part of his assets in this firm, so that his mother's bankruptcy affected him personally only by a loss of eight thousand thalers. In contrast, the greater part of the inheritance he had received from his father remained untouched. Although, as we have seen above, Schopenhauer did not get along exceptionally well with his mother, he offered to share with her and with his sister the part of his fortune that remained intact, but for unknown reasons, they declined this offer.

In general, to the extent that Schopenhauer revered the memory of his father, he treated his mother with coldness and indifference. His biographer Lindner, apparently not without some grounds, supposes that Schopenhauer had his mother precisely in mind in a passage of his *Parerga* where he speaks of women's tendency to extravagance and their incapacity for managing property. Among other things, he says in that chapter:

"All women, with very few exceptions, are inclined to extravagance; therefore, it is urgently necessary to safeguard any existing fortune, except in those rare cases when they themselves have acquired it, from their extravagance. In view of this, I believe that women, whatever their age, can never be regarded as fully of age and must constantly remain under male guardianship, whether that of a father, a husband, a son, or government agents, as we see in India; that they should never be allowed to dispose of property on their own; and that the fact that a mother is appointed, even by force of law, the guardian and administrator of the father's inheritance for her children, I consider a positive absurdity. In most cases, such a woman is capable only of spending with her second husband or lover what the father has with difficulty and care laid by for his children, as even old Homer teaches us. A natural mother after the death of the father of her children often turns into a stepmother to them..." and so on.

After returning from his journey in Italy, Schopenhauer, perhaps in part because of the reduction of his paternal inheritance, decided to seek a professorship. He had in mind three universities: Heidelberg, Göttingen, and Berlin. He wrote to three professors he knew, Ewald, Blumenbach, and Lichtenstein, emphasizing, in accordance with the political conditions of the time, that he intended to adhere strictly to the sphere of speculative philosophy and was far from any thought of influencing the political cast of mind of his contemporaries. He wrote that he had always been concerned, and by the constitution of his mind would be concerned, only with what touches the intellectual activity of people of all epochs and all countries, and that he would consider it beneath him to descend into the interests of a given country or a given epoch. In his deep conviction, such ought to be the views of every true scholar.

In his article "On University Philosophy," printed in the *Parerga*, he says, among other things:

"If the harm done to scholarship by men who are uncalled and incapable consisted only in the fact that they bring it no substantial benefit, as we see with respect to the arts, it would still be tolerable. However, here they do positive harm, first of all in that, in order to uphold what is bad, they enter into a close alliance against everything good and strive in every way to suppress it. Nothing can reconcile them to the superiority of intellect; so it was, so it is, and so it always will be. Furthermore, what a terrible majority is on their side. This is one of the chief obstacles to every kind of progress of mankind."

"People who, instead of studying a philosopher's thoughts," says Schopenhauer elsewhere, "try to familiarize themselves with his biography, resemble those who, instead of looking at a painting, would occupy themselves with its frame, assessing the merits of its carving and the cost of its gilding. However, that is only half the trouble; the trouble is when biographers begin to rummage in your private life and fish out various trifles that have not the slightest relation to a man's scholarly activity."

Schopenhauer himself declined the Heidelberg chair, since rumors reached him of personal quarrels prevailing among the scholarly world there. In Göttingen, he was promised a favorable reception but a minimal number of listeners; therefore, he ultimately chose Berlin, where he arrived in the summer of 1820. There, Schopenhauer hoped to find a sufficient number of both required and voluntary auditors, and he also counted on the fact that, having first become a Privatdozent, he would soon be invited to the chair of philosophy that had become vacant with Solger's death.

Schopenhauer arrived in Berlin not as an unknown beginner but as the author of a significant work, in any case worthy of attention, *The World as Will and Representation*, which had appeared in print about a year and a half earlier. It cannot be said that this work passed unnoticed. In the third volume of the philosophical journal *Hermes*, Professor Herbart published a detailed review of it in which, while differing diametrically from the author in his views, he nevertheless placed him on the same level as Fichte and

Schelling. The well-known Jean Paul Richter wrote of Schopenhauer's work:

"This is a philosophically genial, bold, many-sided work, full of wit and profundity, but often hopelessly and bottomlessly deep, resembling those Norwegian lakes bordered by high sheer cliffs in which the sun is never reflected, over which no bird ever flies, and which are never ruffled by a playful ripple."

Could such a man expect success on the philosophical chair of a German university of that time, permeated with the spirit of philistinism, hazy idealism, and the pursuit of abstraction meant to smooth away unattractive reality? Without denying Schopenhauer a gift for teaching, of which he himself was proud and which impartial contemporaries unanimously note, one nevertheless cannot fail to recognize that by the very content of his teaching, he was as little suited to public activity as, for example, Spinoza. If to this one adds the influence then exercised over young minds by Hegel and Schleiermacher and their less gifted followers, who were clearly hostile to the starting point of Schopenhauer's philosophy, as well as Schopenhauer's stubborn, uncompromising character, one must conclude that from the outset there were very few chances of success for his professorial career.

Already in his trial lecture, delivered, according to the custom of the time, in Latin, he declared that after the true thinker Kant, who had been able to set philosophy on the right path, the arena of philosophy had been clogged by sophists who discredited philosophy and discouraged serious study of it. However, an avenger would soon appear who would restore this discredited philosophy to all its rights. Among the papers left after Schopenhauer's death were found outlines of his Berlin lectures, showing how conscientiously he approached the task he had undertaken. However, there is no doubt that his philosophy did not suit the "Young Germany" of that day, with its rather peculiar political and scholarly ideals. He soon became convinced of this, and after a relatively unsuccessful year of teaching, in the spring of 1822, he shook the university dust from his feet and again set off traveling in the southern European countries so dear to him. In Berlin, Schopenhauer disliked everything: university morals, climate, and way of life. During his stay, he moved very little in the university sphere. He deliberately avoided his competitors in philosophy, for the pedantry of the scholarly world was simply repugnant to him. He became closer with several members of fashionable society, though even there, he was highly selective in acquaintances.

Berlin became especially hateful to him after

a tragicomic episode that occurred there during his brief professorship. The matter, petty enough, irritated Schopenhauer for a long time. It was as follows. In August 1821, an acquaintance of his landlady, Mrs. Becker, a seamstress named Carolina Marquet, brought Arthur Schopenhauer to court for insult by word and deed. In Schopenhauer's written response to the plaintiff's complaint, we find the following account of this absurd affair:

"The accusation brought against me," writes Schopenhauer, "is a monstrous weaving together of lies with truth. For sixteen months, I have occupied a furnished apartment from the widow Becker, consisting of a study and a bedroom. Adjacent to the bedroom is a small closet, which I used at first, but later, I no longer needed it, so I yielded to the landlady. For the last five months, this closet has been occupied by my present accuser. The anteroom of the apartment, however, has always been for the exclusive use of myself and another lodger, and apart from the two of us and our occasional guests, no one was supposed to appear in the anteroom. However, about two weeks before August 12, returning home, I found in the anteroom three unknown women. For many reasons, I did not like this, and, calling the landlady, I asked whether she had allowed Mrs. Marquet to sit in my anteroom. She replied that she had not, that Marquet in general did not go from her closet into other rooms, and that in general Marquet had no business in my anteroom.

"On August 12, coming home, I again found in the anteroom three women. Learning that the landlady was not at home, I myself ordered them to leave. Two obeyed without objection; the accuser did not, declaring that she was a respectable person. Having repeated to Mrs. Marquet the order to depart, I went into my rooms. After remaining there for some time, intending to go out again, I came back into the anteroom with my hat on and a stick in my hand. Seeing that Mrs. Marquet was still there, I repeated my request that she leave, but she stubbornly wished to remain in the anteroom. Then I threatened to throw her out, and since she persisted, I in fact threw her out the door. She raised a cry, threatened me with court, and demanded her things, which I threw out to her. However, then, under the pretext that some rag of hers remained in the anteroom unnoticed by me, she again intruded into my rooms. I pushed her out again, though she resisted with all her strength and cried loudly, wishing to attract the other lodgers. When I was expelling her the second time, she fell, most likely intentionally. However, her assertions that I tore off her cap and trampled her with my feet are pure lies. Such a wild assault is incompatible with my character, my social position, and my upbringing. After removing Marquet beyond the door, I did not touch her again, only sent a strong word after her. In that, of course, I was at fault and am liable to punishment. In all the rest, not at all, since I exercised only the incontestable right to protect my dwelling from impudent encroachments. If she ended up with abrasions and bruises, I permit myself to doubt that they were obtained in this encounter, but even in the latter case, she has only herself to blame. Such insignificant injuries risk anyone who lays siege to another's doors."

In the first instance, the plaintiff's claim was dismissed. However, the court of the second instance overturned the acquittal of Schopenhauer, who at that time was traveling in Switzerland, and sentenced him to pay a fine of twenty thalers and to compensate Marquet for damages, as security for which an attachment was placed on Schopenhauer's funds held by the banker Mendelssohn. The case dragged through various instances until 1826 and ended in Schopenhauer's being required to pay Marquet a life pension of sixty thalers a year. He paid this pension for twenty whole years, until 1846, when the old woman finally died. On the certificate of Marquet's death, which freed him from further payment of the life pension, Schopenhauer wrote the following inscription: "Obit anus, abit onus" ("The old woman is gone, the burden has gone").

In the spring of 1822, while his lawsuit with the old woman Marquet was still pending, Schopenhauer, having renounced the Berlin professorship, set off traveling, first to Switzerland and then to Italy, where he spent the autumn in Venice and Milan and the winter in Florence. In the spring of 1823, the philosopher traveled from Italy through the Tyrol to Munich, where he lived for about a year. In Italy, as during his first journey, he preferred the company of Englishmen and carefully avoided Germans. In Munich, Schopenhauer suffered a severe illness, as a result of which he became almost entirely deaf in one ear, and from there, in the summer of 1824, he went to Gastein for treatment. From Gastein, he returned to Dresden, which was dear to him from earlier memories. Naturally, neither the nature of Saxony nor the manner of life in the Saxon capital could have changed sharply in the last ten years. However, many of his former good acquaintances, Schopenhauer no longer found there; and above all, his own personal mood was no longer what it had been. He had ceased to expect a great future for himself and, not finding complete inner peace, conceived the idea of translating the works of remarkable but little-known thinkers of past times more or less close to him in spirit, hoping thereby to prepare the public to assimilate his own philosophical views. With this aim, Schopenhauer set about producing a popular exposition of David Hume's philosophical writings, even writing a long preface. For unknown reasons the planned translation did not materialize, which, as Schopenhauer's biographer Frauenstädt writes, "cannot but be regretted, since, given Schopenhauer's undoubted ability as a translator, of which the occasional passages from English writers inserted into the text of his works give clear evidence, his translation of Hume would also have been exemplary, all the more since Hume, like Voltaire, belongs among the writers most akin to Schopenhauer in spirit and therefore most frequently cited by him. I remember well from conversations with Schopenhauer that he recommended I read Hume's dialogues."

Schopenhauer's translation of Hume remained unfinished because of his sudden departure for Berlin, caused by the above-mentioned lawsuit with Mrs. Marquet, which he had won in the first instance. Around the same time came his second attempt to lecture at the University of Berlin, now as a Privatdozent. This attempt too failed: among those enrolled in his course, there were very few actual students; mostly, there were various dilettantes. Annoyed, Schopenhauer closed his course and once and for all renounced academic teaching. However, he continued to live in Berlin, zealously studying, among other things, Spanish and translating some of his favorite English poets into German. This period of his Berlin life also includes his acquaintance with Alexander von Humboldt, in whom Schopenhauer acknowledged more learning than intellect.

Finally, in 1831, the cholera raging in Berlin forced Schopenhauer to leave that city for good. He decided to settle not in northern Germany, where he was born and where he had spent most of his life up to maturity, but in the south, choosing Frankfurt am Main as his place of residence. From there, he moved for a short time to Mannheim, but in 1833, he returned to Frankfurt and thereafter lived in that city almost without leaving it for twenty-eight years.

# Chapter: IV

**Schopenhauer's appearance and manners – His favorite replies – A letter to the typesetter – Correspondence with Brockhaus – Schopenhauer on table turning – His view of suicide – His manner of life – Schopenhauer's illness and death – His funeral – Gwinner's graveside address – A monument on Schopenhauer's grave – The dimensions of Schopenhauer's skull**

Biographers describe Schopenhauer's appearance as follows. He was somewhat below average height, strongly built, slender, and with an enormous head; but most remarkable were his light, shining, blue eyes, which, during his many wanderings, attracted the attention of people entirely unknown to him. Some found in him a certain resemblance to Beethoven; others asserted that his face, and especially the outline of his mouth, recalled Voltaire. He always dressed with extreme elegance, though, contrary to contemporary fashions, he retained the cut of clothing of the early nineteenth century. Not very sociable even in youth, after his university failures, he shunned socicty still more. Having settled permanently in Frankfurt am Main, he tried to keep as far as possible from local interests, forming few ties with the people around him. He could not endure not only fashionable conversation but even everyday talk; yet when he had to speak in company, he never spoke in abstract phrases. His conversational speech was as simple, vivid, clear, precise, and lively as his style. Having managed to avoid the petty interests, cares, joys, and sorrows of family life, and relating rather indifferently to the phenomena of public life, he concentrated all the powers of his mind on what in antiquity was called dialectic, that is, the art of conducting conversation exclusively within the sphere of pure thought. At the same time, he proceeded from the principle that depth of thought not only does not exclude beauty of expression but, on the contrary, gains from it. However one-sided the thoughts he expressed may at times have seemed, it was impossible not to acknowledge the highly persuasive manner in which he presented them.

Schopenhauer, planning a complete edition of his works, intended to place as its epigraph the words "Non multa." This epigraph truly characterizes him as a scholar. Schopenhauer knew many, but not many things. Neither his reading nor his knowledge astonished by sheer extent. From youth, he was accustomed to limit his scholarly studies to comparatively few, but fundamental works. Thus, for example, he scarcely followed the contemporary literature of his day in all its branches. However, if he read something, he read it thoroughly and attentively and mastered his subject completely. The very fact that he read slowly shows that he was not able to read a great deal in quantity. He maintained that one should not read bad books, because such books steal from a person his most precious possession: time. He preferred books in foreign languages to German ones and most willingly read the Greek and Latin classics. Already while studying the ancient languages, Schopenhauer read the most notable classics, and later familiarized himself with others. He reread Plato and Aristotle many times. Among the Romans, his favorite writer was Seneca. In general, he carefully avoided learning about the writers of the classical world secondhand, from histories of literature. He was especially outraged by the manner in which many philosophers of his time acquainted themselves with the thinkers of antiquity, not firsthand but from secondhand accounts. In his conviction, Fichte, Schelling, and Hegel did so. This unwillingness to receive knowledge secondhand also led him, as far as possible, to avoid translations. He demanded of an accurate scholar acquaintance at least with the most important literary languages, although this did not prevent him from engaging in translation at times. Anyone not acquainted with Latin, Schopenhauer was simply regarded as uneducated. Of modern literature, he most willingly occupied himself with English, and here his thorough knowledge of English was beneficial. He felt a special attraction to ascetic and mystical literature, and for a time even studied the German mystics with care. Any phenomenon akin to Buddhism on European soil drew his attention. His biographer Gwinner gives the following interesting list of world works that constituted Schopenhauer's favorite reading: Seneca's 105th letter, the beginning of Hobbes's *De Cive*, Machiavelli's *The Prince*, Polonius's address to Laertes in *Hamlet*, Gracián's *Maxims*, the French moralists, Shinston, and Klinger.

Throughout his life, Schopenhauer regarded the great poets of all times and peoples with extraordinary sympathy and respect. Most often, he read Shakespeare and Goethe, then Calderón and Byron. He especially admired Byron's *Cain*, evidently because of the pessimistic spirit that permeates this work. Among lyric poets, after Petrarch, he rated Burns and Bürger especially highly. For the latter, for the immediacy and power of his lyricism, he was ready to assign a place directly after Goethe. Schopenhauer also treated Schiller with respect, not following in this regard the example of the *esprits forts* [freethinkers (Fr.)] of his era. Second- and third-rate poets, he did not read at all, finding that it was not worth spending time on them. His colossal memory helped him assimilate thoroughly the mass of what he read.

However, Schopenhauer drew his knowledge far from books alone. Accustomed from his youth to observe the world around him, the famous philosopher constantly broadened his intellectual horizon, seeking grains of truth wherever there was even the slightest hope of finding them. He carefully watched every heavenly or earthly phenomenon, and for the most part sharply diverged from accepted opinion. Often, what attracted others and what they considered supremely important, he left wholly without attention, and conversely, what others ignored or mocked acquired the most tremendous significance in his eyes.

Schopenhauer led an extraordinarily regular way of life. If he recognized something as reasonable and introduced it into his domestic routine, he did not cease to adhere to it with pedantic strictness. There are people who cannot profit from their experience. For Schopenhauer, every new experience, in whatever sphere, became a guiding principle for his further actions, and he continued in a given direction with iron consistency. Schopenhauer rose in summer and winter between seven and eight in the morning and drank coffee, which he prepared for himself. His housekeeper was strictly ordered not even to appear in his study in the mornings, since he considered the morning hours, when the brain has rested sufficiently, the best working time and tolerated not the slightest disturbance. He worked steadily until half past twelve, then played the flute for about half an hour, and precisely at one o'clock went to a restaurant to dine. All his life, he never kept a household of his own and remained faithful to his restaurant dinners. However, he rarely took part in general table conversation. After dinner, he returned home, drank coffee, rested for an hour or so, and then engaged in comparatively lighter reading. Toward evening, he went for a walk outside the city, choosing mainly the most secluded paths; only in bad weather did he walk on the city boulevards. His gait remained light and elastic until old age. He liked to walk alone, in order to be as close as possible to nature and as far as possible from human society. He loved nature, understood it, and expressed this understanding in many scattered remarks throughout his works. "How beautiful nature is," Schopenhauer exclaims, for example, in one note. "Any uncultivated, neglected spot, that is, a place left to itself, which man does not touch with his clumsy paw, nature at once adorns with the greatest taste, clothing it with plants, flowers, and shrubs whose natural grace and elegant grouping clearly testify that they did not grow under the stick of the great egoist called man." In summer, he undertook longer walks, though never lasting more than a day. Extensive journeys, which he had liked so much in youth, he considered in old age useless and even inappropriate. The philosopher maliciously ridiculed the newest, purposeless passion for travel, this "riding back and forth under the pretext of rest." In the last period of his life, he never went farther than Mainz, where he sometimes visited an old friend, and the nearby Taunus hills.

After his walk, Schopenhauer went to his study to read. From youth, he had formed the habit, if not of reading, then at least of skimming the *Times* every day. In addition, he looked through some English and French journals. Among German periodicals, he usually read the *Göttingen Learned Notices*, the *Heidelberg Yearbook*, and the *Literary Supplement* of the well-known Wolfgang Menzel, who pleased him because he "knows how to write entertaining and instructive reviews like the English and French, whereas German critics and reviewers only cast a fog over the reader and tire him." The reviewer's task, in his opinion, should consist in conveying as accurately as possible the content of a book, to spare the reader the labor of reading the book itself. He was especially angered by the ever more widespread corruption of the German language in the German press through various barbarisms. "A German," he used to say, "is incapable of preserving even that one treasure of his of which he has the right to be proud."

In his correspondence, despite seriousness and even an apparent severity, Schopenhauer appears as a man of the sharpest wit. Preparing, for example, to proceed with the second edition of his work *The World as Will and Representation*, he wrote the following witty letter to his typesetter:

"My dear Mr. Typesetter. We relate to each other as soul to body. Therefore, following the example of those, we must render each other mutual support in order to create a work that would make the heart of Mr. Brockhaus (the publisher) rejoice. To that end, I have done everything that depended on me, and on every line, at every word, even at every letter, I thought of you, whether you would be able to read what is written. Now you too do what depends on you. My manuscript is written not in an elegant but in an apparent hand. The careful finishing of my work made many insertions necessary. However, with every insertion, it is clearly marked where it belongs, so that you cannot go wrong in this respect, provided you are sufficiently attentive. You are convinced that everything is in order and that you need only find for every sign in the margins the corresponding word. I also ask you to pay due attention to my spelling and punctuation, and please do not imagine that you understand these matters better than I do. I repeat: I am the soul and you are the body. If you come upon a crossed-out line anywhere, look more closely to see whether there is in that line a word not crossed out. By no means allow the supposition that an oversight could have occurred on my part. If you do not wish to create extra proof-correcting work for yourself, then spare me the necessity of making numerous corrections on the proof sheets."

Not without interest is also his correspondence with the bookseller Brockhaus concerning the second edition in 1843 of the first volume of his *Die Welt als Wille...* and the publication of the second volume of the same work. He wrote:

"You will, I hope, find it entirely natural that I turn to you with the proposal that you publish the second volume of my *World as Will and Representation*, just completed by me. Perhaps you will be surprised that I finished it only twenty-four years after the first, although all this time I have not ceased working on it. However, what is meant to exist long is created slowly. Its final revision is the labor of the last four years, and I undertook it after convincing myself that it is time for me to finish. I have just passed my fifty-fifth year, which means I am entering an age when life becomes more and more problematic. Even if it should still last, mental powers nevertheless begin to weaken. This second volume has considerable advantages over the first and relates to it as a finished painting to a mere sketch. The advantage consists in the solidity and richness of thought and knowledge that can appear only as the fruit of an entire life spent in intense study and reflection. In any case, this volume is the best of everything I have ever written. It even eclipses the significance of the first volume. In addition, I have now been able to express myself much more freely and directly than twenty-four years ago, partly because the times themselves have changed, partly because my decisive renunciation of the professorship and of university scholarship has untied my hands. I very much wish that you would decide to reprint the first volume as well, so that a work whose significance and merits have not yet been recognized, appearing in a new and improved form, might attract the deserved attention of the public, which is especially desirable at present, when the decline of religious feeling strengthens the demand for philosophy and consequently increases interest in it, and yet what could satisfy this demand is lacking. The works of so-called philosophers are least capable of achieving this goal. Therefore, I find the time as convenient as possible to come forward again with my work, and it is most opportune that I have completed the second volume precisely now. However, I will still be treated with the same injustice as before. Literary history teaches us precisely that all solid, enduring works were at first neglected, like mine, whereas mediocrity enjoyed undeserved attention and honor. My time must come someday, and it will come. The question of paying me any honorarium I leave to your discretion. I did not work for money. On the other hand, I understand very well that the costs of printing and paper for so large a work will be considerable and can be covered only over a sufficiently long period. I repeat: I leave it to you to set the conditions of this edition. I have already acquired some public, and in time that 'some public' will become a very numerous public, and my work will see many editions, though I will hardly live to see them."

When Brockhaus answered Schopenhauer's proposal with a refusal, the Frankfurt philosopher-hermit wrote to him:

"Your refusal was for me as unexpected as it

was painful. I wished to make the public a gift, and a very valuable one, but in addition to paying you myself for this gift, it is already too much. If matters have indeed come to the point that no publisher can be found who would risk the printing expenses for the publication of the work of my whole life, while Hegelian nonsense goes through several editions, then let my work appear in a posthumous edition, when the generation is born that will joyfully greet my every line. Furthermore, that time will come."

In the end, Schopenhauer reached an agreement with Brockhaus, and the latter printed both volumes of his *World as Will and Representation* on the conditions Schopenhauer proposed.

When, in the 1850s, table turning came into fashion, Schopenhauer treated this strange fad with complete seriousness, yet with his characteristic wit managed to give even this absurdity a serious philosophical underpinning. In April 1852, Schopenhauer wrote to Lindner: "The table turning that has lately come into fashion will someday bring a complete triumph to my philosophy. I am deeply convinced that the force acting in this case is by no means electricity, as some suppose, but precisely the will, which manifests here its magical properties, influencing not only its own body but also foreign bodies. The table moves, obeying the unanimous will of all who touch it. This is the most brilliant confirmation of what I long ago stated in my work *On the Will in Nature,* namely, in the chapter 'On Animal Magnetism and Magic.' If, however, in this case people talk about electricity, this happens because of the absurd habit of our quasi-scholars of attributing to the force of electricity everything that appears to them obscure and inexplicable."

Schopenhauer's view of suicide, expressed in one of his letters to Lindner, is also interesting: "A man who resorts to suicide proves only that he does not understand a joke, that, like a bad player, he does not know how to lose calmly and, when a bad card comes to him, prefers to throw up the game and, in annoyance, rise from the table."

Schopenhauer was extremely calculating in money matters, and thanks to his prudence and frugality, he managed almost to double the fortune inherited from his father, which had suffered considerably in his youth. In the last years of his life, his writings brought him a significant income, writings for which in earlier years he had difficulty finding even publishers willing to print them without payment. He joked that "most people earn their money in youth and middle age, whereas I earn mine at an age when other people already stop earning money." He lived very simply and only at the age of fifty acquired his own furniture. Apparently, he felt no need for remarkable comfort or aesthetic refinement in his surroundings. The best and largest room of his apartment was occupied by his remarkable library. On a marble stand in that room, in which he also died, stood a real gilded statuette of Buddha. On his writing desk was a bust of Kant. Above the sofa hung an oil portrait of Goethe. On the other walls were portraits of Kant, Descartes, Shakespeare, several family portraits, and portraits of himself taken at various ages.

Until the last year of his life, Schopenhauer enjoyed remarkable health. Only a few years before his death, he fainted at the table, though without any dire consequences. However, in April 1860, returning home after dinner with his usual brisk pace, he suddenly felt palpitations and tightness in the chest. These symptoms recurred several times during the summer and sometimes forced him to stop in the streets. Since he could not free himself from the habit of walking very fast, he found it necessary to shorten his walks. Once, in August, in the morning, he had an especially severe suffocating attack, in consequence of which he nearly choked. Schopenhauer felt an aversion to all kinds of medicines and called foolish those who imagined that one could buy lost health for money in pharmacies. In the first days of September, the attack recurred, and the admirer Gwinner, who lived in Frankfurt and was summoned to him on the morning of September 9, at once became convinced that Schopenhauer had pneumonia. Schopenhauer immediately declared that his end was approaching. However, a few hours after the crisis passed, he recovered so much that he could get out of bed and receive visitors. Ten days later, however, he had another attack. That evening, Gwinner came to him. He was sitting on the sofa and complaining of palpitations; yet his voice was strong and ringing. Gwinner found the sick man reading Disraeli's *Curiosities of Literature*. Opening to the place where Disraeli speaks of writers who ruined their publishers, Schopenhauer remarked jokingly: "Our dear professors of philosophy almost brought me to that as well." He then said that the thought that worms would soon gnaw his body did not trouble him in the least, but that he could not think without horror of how the gentlemen professors of philosophy would gnaw at his mind. He was very interested in the affairs of Italy, then in the process of unification. However, he expressed, very aptly and apparently with justice, the fear that a unified, leveled Italy would play a more minor role in the intellectual life of Europe than the Italy politically divided had played. In the course of conversation, the sick man said that it would be very inopportune for him to die just then, since he had only just conceived the idea of seriously revising and supplementing his *Parerga und Paralipomena*. "Besides," he said, "if formerly I desired the longest possible life for energetic struggle with my enemies, now I would gladly live on in order at least in old age to enjoy the recognition of my scholarly merits which has made me wait so long, but now reaches me from everywhere." Schopenhauer rejoiced that he was beginning to be understood and valued not only by professional scholars but also by so-called dilettantes. Among other things, he read Gwinner excerpts from sympathetic letters he had just received from various places, from people entirely unknown to him.

"In general," says Gwinner, "during this last conversation of ours, Schopenhauer was as sociable and gentle as I had never seen him. Leaving the sick man for fear of tiring him too much, I was far from suspecting that I had seen him for the last time, that I had for the last time shaken his hand. Taking leave of me, Schopenhauer said quite seriously that it would be a true blessing for him to become nothing, but that, unfortunately, there was as yet little hope of that. 'In any case,' he added, 'come what may, my intellectual conscience is clean and calm.'"

Two days later, on the morning of September 20, Schopenhauer had such severe spasms in his chest that he fell to the floor and bruised his forehead. During the day, he recovered somewhat and spent the night relatively quietly. On September 21, Schopenhauer rose at his usual time and sat down on the sofa to drink coffee. However, when a few minutes later the doctor entered the room, he found him fallen back against the sofa, lifeless. Paralysis of the lungs ended his life. His face breathed calm, and there were no traces of death agony. He had always counted on an easy death, asserting that he who has lived his whole life in solitude will be better able than anyone else to depart into eternal solitude, in the joyful consciousness that he is returning to where he came from so richly endowed and in the confidence that he has honestly and conscientiously fulfilled his calling.

In accordance with his expressed written wish, no autopsy was performed. His brow was crowned with a laurel wreath. On September 26, the mortal remains of Schopenhauer were committed to the earth. His pupil and later biographer, Gwinner, delivered the following graveside address over his teacher's grave:

"The coffin of this remarkable man, who lived for about thirty years among us and yet remained for us as it were a foreigner, calls forth special reflections. None of those standing here is bound to him by ties of blood. He lived alone and died alone. However, I will allow myself to say that the deceased found some compensation for his solitude. That passionate desire to know the eternal, which in most people appears only in view of approaching death, was the constant companion of his whole life. Being a fervent worshiper of truth, taking life with the utmost seriousness, he from his youth became accustomed to turn away without ceremony from every lie and pretense, not fearing the risk of repelling people and spoiling relations with them. This thinking and deeply feeling man lived his whole life alone, misunderstood, remaining faithful to himself. His free mind did not bow under the burdens of life. Richly endowed by fate, he strove all his life to be worthy of these gifts and, keeping in view his high calling, was always ready to renounce everything that gladdens the hearts of other people. For many, many years, his contemporaries refused to give him his due justice. The laurels that now adorn his brow came to him only in his last hour. However, faith in his calling never ceased to take root in his soul. Through long years of undeserved solitude, he did not retreat a single step from the road he had marked out for himself and grew gray in unwavering service to his beloved truth, ever mindful of the words of the Old Testament: 'Great is the power of truth, and it will prevail in the end.' Those of us who had the good fortune to stand closer to the 'Frankfurt sage' will never forget his clear, bright gaze, his lively, convinced speech. A guarantee that this man will not be forgotten is that throughout his life, he stubbornly refused to walk the ordinary path. His teaching will stand unshaken even when all traces of this grave we have just dug have long since disappeared. Many saw in him only a misanthrope, but however low an opinion he had of man, he sympathized with people and felt compassion for them. Fate did not grant him the opportunity to found his own home, to acquire a family. However, he has built an edifice whose doors he has flung wide open before all thinking humanity."

Schopenhauer's grave is adorned with a simple stone slab entwined with ivy. On this slab, only two words are carved: Arthur Schopenhauer, and nothing more: neither the year of his birth nor the year of his death nor any other inscription. This was done at his expressly stated wish before death, since he proceeded from the conviction that everything else concerning his personality and activity was for posterity to know. When Gwinner once asked him where he wished to be buried, Schopenhauer answered: "It is all the same; they will know how to find me."

Let us note, however, that very recently the *Frankfurter Zeitung* published an article urging the opening of a subscription for the erection of a monument to Schopenhauer.

German newspapers also report that, in connection with September 21 of the present year, marking the expiration of the thirty-year term established by German laws for the heirs' right to the literary property of a deceased writer, it is proposed to proceed with a new complete edition of Schopenhauer's works.

Let us add, in supplement to these brief biographical data about Schopenhauer's life, that as the model taken from his head after death shows, his skull was of extraordinary size, surpassing the skulls of Kant, Schiller, Napoleon I, and Talleyrand. Perhaps these unusual dimensions of the skull may serve as some indication that, in the author of *The World as Will and Representation*, intellect stood in the foreground and feeling in the background.

# Chapter: V

**Distinctive features of Schopenhauer's philosophical world view – What does Schopenhauer mean by the word "will"? – Will and reason – The three fundamental properties of will: identity, immutability, freedom – Will as representation** – *On the Will in Nature* – **Experience as the foundation of philosophy – The meaning and role of metaphysics – Schopenhauer's view of psychology**

Schopenhauer's philosophy stands in sharp contradiction to the metaphysical views of his three famous contemporaries: Fichte, Schelling, and Hegel. He distinguishes two worlds, two spheres: on the one hand, the world as appearance, as representation, and above it, separated from it by a whole abyss, the real world, the world as will. The first is subject to causality, like everything that exists in time and space. The second is free and beyond all constraint, standing outside time and space. To distinguish these two worlds carefully, to define their boundaries precisely, to make them accessible to sight and hearing, is, in Schopenhauer's opinion, the philosopher's first task, and this is what he set himself on the very first page of his major work, *The World as Will and Representation*. "The world is my representation," he begins, concentrating in these four words both the idealist philosophy of India and the essence of the modern systems of Leibniz, Berkeley, Hume, and Kant. What could be simpler and more indisputable than this basic formula? The eye sees colors, the ear hears sounds, the hand feels surfaces and bodies. However, we do not know forms, sounds, or colors in themselves. We know only the organs that present them: "all this is only represented" to us. Thus, the world, as something represented, is not something real: in the world of phenomena, everything is only seeming. However, the world consists of two halves, two hemispheres: one is the realm of visibility, which contains nothing real; the other, unexplored and mysterious in its essence, is will.

To avoid further misunderstanding, it must be noted that Schopenhauer gives the word "will" not its everyday meaning but a wholly special one. Here, it is not a matter of will as something rational and conscious, but of will as something instinctive, analogous to the desire to live or the instinct of self-preservation, in short, will in the broadest sense of the word. "Outside will and cognition," says Schopenhauer, "not only is nothing known to us, but nothing can even be thought. It is impossible to seek reality for application to the bodily world in anything else." This will, this striving, must be strictly distinguished from the consciousness that accompanies it and from the motive that determines it – all that is not the essence of will but only its manifestation. Thus, for example, if I say that the force that makes a stone gravitate toward the earth is, in itself, outside any representation, this does not mean that the stone moves by virtue of some conscious motive known to it, since in that latter form it will manifest itself only in man.

In Schopenhauer's view, will (striving) possesses the following three basic properties: identity, immutability, and freedom.

Although will can be traced everywhere, it is most easily discovered in man and in human consciousness. It constitutes the foundation of psychology, for the true, indestructible essence of man is will. Schopenhauer proves the predominance of will over consciousness. The latter is something physical; will is something metaphysical. Consciousness is manifestation; will is essence. Consciousness is something accidental; will is something unshakable. Consciousness is light; will is warmth. Will is the prototype of all knowing; it makes itself felt everywhere and in everything. Will is primary, reason secondary. Will is immutable, reason subject to change. Will can drown out, paralyze, and confuse reason, and it can also raise and exalt it. Reason is the head, will is the heart.

The distinction between will and knowing is without doubt the culminating point of Schopenhauer's philosophy and the newest side of his doctrine. However, contrary to other thinkers, he assigns first place to will, understood in the sense indicated, and second place to reason. Reason in man, and to a certain extent in animals as well, is only a product of will; even at the highest point of its manifestation, it appears only after will. Thus, it is not man's primary, essential state but only secondary and accidental. Reason perishes with man, but will remains. "For me," says Schopenhauer, "what is eternal and indestructible in man is not the soul, but, using a chemical term, the base of the soul, that is, will."

One may say that Schopenhauer proves that the will does not change in the world. It always remains the same, being completely identical both in a man and in a tick. For if an insect desires something, it desires it just as decisively as man does. The only difference lies in the object of desire, in the motive of desire, and in the understanding that illumines this desire. The order of nature is immutable, and this immutability does not depend on reason. Reason is something mobile and capricious, something that introduces infinite variety into the world. However, the organ of will, the heart, is something constant, not changing with time and place. Therefore, the measure must be will, that is, what is identical and immutable, and not reason, something mobile and changing. Will is the measure of life.

Finally, will, striving, is free, both physically and morally. It depends on itself whether to affirm or to deny itself, and in this lies the basis of the highest morality, the morality that gives birth to heroes and saints. However, of course, this free will must not be understood in the sense of mere "arbitrariness."

Schopenhauer himself considers it an exceptional merit that he decomposed the human "I" into will and representation. "Lavoisier," he says, "decomposed water into hydrogen and oxygen and thus created a new era in physics and chemistry. I, however, decomposed the soul or spirit into two very different constituent elements: will and representation. All metaphysical systems up to now proceeded either from matter, resulting in materialism, or from spirit, leading to spiritualism. However, both, in their further conclusions, led to absurdities and proved untenable. I assign to one component of the soul or spirit, will, first place; to what is to be known, second place. Matter is an unavoidable correlate of the knowing subject, since matter is unthinkable without representation, but representation is also unthinkable without matter. Matter as such exists only in representation, and the capacity for representation is conceivable only as one of the properties of the organism.

The beginning of philosophy and its possibility lie in man himself, but not because, as Schopenhauer's predecessors taught, he thinks (Descartes: 'Je pense, donc je suis' [I think, therefore I am (Fr.)]), but because at the same time he wills. If man only thought, then the forms of intuition and above all the chain of motives and actions, causes and effects, would be for him as reliable a guiding thread as, for example, observation and the instinct arising from it are for an animal. However, man not only thinks, but he also wills. Hence, the fundamental question: how can the ideal and the real side of man's psychic activity exist together and simultaneously, representation and will? He seeks this connection of the external (representation) with the internal (will) by considering every movement, in its external manifestation, a mere representation, and calling what underlies this phenomenon an inner cause, even in so-called dead nature, will. He uses our twofold knowledge of ourselves and of everything around us, given in two entirely different ways, as a key to explaining the essence of every phenomenon of nature. Even where the most apparent cause produces a given effect, there still exists something mysterious, some X that constitutes the very essence, the motive of the phenomenon, which is accessible to us only as representation. This X in all the phenomena we observe is identical with what, in the actions of our body, we mean by the word 'will.'"

These general theses, first set forth by Schopenhauer in *The World as Will and Representation*, he later developed in greater detail, though not as convincingly and somewhat paradoxically, in his work *On the Will in Nature*, published in 1836, and in the *Supplements* published in 1844. There, he proceeds from the proposition that man cannot know everything; omniscience is a lie. Philosophy must honestly reconcile itself with this basic proposition, and, not chasing the unattainable, sincerely and simply enter the path of experience, in order to create a metaphysics grounded in observation and intuition rather than in pure ideas, a metaphysics that would seek to embrace the totality of experience rather than this or that part of it. Even with such a restriction, the sphere of philosophy will remain broad enough.

This philosophy, in general, philosophy in the metaphysical sense, differs significantly from the special philosophy of each science. The special sciences have as their object establishing the connection between phenomena according to the law of causality that rules the entire realm of phenomena. They limit themselves to stating causal connections between various phenomena. Each stops where the establishment and explanation of this connection ends, without entering into consideration of the essence of things as something inexplicable and unknowable. Philosophy begins where the sciences stop. It presupposes nothing known. It wishes and is obliged to explain everything, both the mutual connection of phenomena and the bonds of causality on which this connection depends. What other sciences presuppose, what they take as a basis for their explanations, is precisely the material of the philosophical problem.

Each science has its own philosophy, which is only a generalization and coordination of its main results considered as a whole. These main general results provide data for philosophy in the narrow sense, freeing it from the necessity of seeking them out in each separate science. Thus, the philosophies of the special sciences are, in a sense, intermediaries between the sciences and philosophy in general. The latter finds in them confirmation and verification, since general truth can be confirmed only by particular truths. However significant the advantages of the division of empirical labor, however significant the results of the special sciences, it is necessary that they become the property of philosophy.

Since experience is the criterion of truth, philosophy must begin with inner experience or cognition. Descartes and Bacon already understood this. In Bacon's view, philosophy rests on experience, not on producing one or another experiment as the other sciences do. However, in general experience, that is, on the essence of its content, on its inner and outer elements, and finally on its form and material. From this, it becomes clear that above all, one must observe the medium of experience, its form, and nature. This medium is Schopenhauer's representation, or what others call "cognition." Therefore, every philosophy must begin with studying the laws and forms of cognition, its value, and the limits that constrain it. This investigation constitutes the first stage of philosophy (*philosophia prima*), which falls into two parts. One concerns primary representations created through intuition and could be called a theory of understanding. The other deals with secondary, abstract representations and the laws governing them. This is logic, or the theory of reason.

Metaphysics, in Schopenhauer's view, must explain the entire realm of experience, but only from a standpoint higher than empirical science, without, however, going beyond the bounds of experience. Finally, it must explain what other sciences are not able to explain. To achieve this aim, it combines inner experience with outer experience, with a conception of the phenomenon taken as a whole in its various senses, in its inner connection and complexity. In Schopenhauer's opinion, Kant was wrong to declare metaphysics impossible. He was wrong in that, having taken experience as a starting point, he asserted that metaphysics has nothing in common with experience, thereby opening wide access to skepticism.

However, while restoring, in refutation of Kant, the possibility of metaphysics, Schopenhauer, sharply diverging here from Hegel, wishes to delimit its boundaries strictly. He does not in the least claim to explain everything by its means, to find a corresponding "why" and "how" for everything. Man is surrounded by profound darkness. Our understanding is very imperfect. Our intellect often deceives us and misleads us. However, by adhering strictly to experience, taking as a starting point living intuition and not dead abstraction, we may hope to clarify something in this darkness. We will be able to understand, of course, not nature itself, but what is in nature, and that already means something. Proceeding slowly and cautiously, we pass from phenomenon to reality, from what appears to what must appear, in short, to metaphysics, to a metaphysics not foggy, abstract, and presumptuous, but to the only real and true metaphysics, which is the totality of experience.

Schopenhauer views the life of the soul not from a materialist standpoint. He does not see it as only a product of atoms of matter acting mechanically and chemically. On the other hand, he does not view it from a purely spiritual standpoint. He sees in it a manifestation of the forces of nature, in which the most essential of every force of nature, will, appears in a higher degree than in other manifestations of the forces of nature that are exclusively mechanical and chemical. These higher forces of nature are indeed connected with the lower ones and need them, but at the same time rise above them and use them for their own ends. In Schopenhauer's view, what should be regarded as accurate and enduring in materialism is the explanation of all kinds of activity, both higher and lower, by means of forces inherent in nature as manifestations of nature's activity. What is false and untenable is the desire to abolish all distinction among the forces of nature, reducing the highly diverse world of phenomena to a gray monotony of matter acting only mechanically.

Life, in Schopenhauer's words, is one of the functions of an organism formed by the vital force, or what is the same, by the desire to live. Within organic life, the role of the soul as one of the brain's functions comes into its own only when the organism, due to more complex needs, begins to feel the need for an apparatus that would regulate its relations to the external world and direct its steps within it. Just as everything that exists is given specific organs for defense and attack, so the will to live is given reason as a means for preserving the individual and the species. Reason is placed in the service of will. Only in exceptional cases does reason exceed the measure required by its role as the servant of will, emancipates itself from that role, and rises to the level of genius, contemplating the world in a purely objective manner.

This Schopenhauerian explanation of the life and activity of the soul can by no means be called materialistic, though it cannot be called spiritualistic either. The soul, according to Schopenhauer's figurative representation, is a lamp that the desire to live, manifesting itself in the organism, lights for itself in order to find its way in the external world. It is the guide and counselor of will. Thus, Schopenhauer successfully avoids a spiritualist dualism between body and soul, man and animal. Matter as phenomenon he derives from representation. Representation itself he derives from the real side of matter, from will, in the form in which the latter manifests itself at the level of animal existence.

In this program, sketched in general outline, there is no place for so-called rational psychology. Indeed, Schopenhauer refuses to assign the latter a place among the metaphysical sciences, leaving that "to philistines and Hegelians." Proceeding from the view that man's true essence cannot be understood otherwise than in the totality of the world, that microcosm and macrocosm explain each other and are even identical, he does not recognize the necessity of a separate science of the soul. He would rather replace such a science with a broad anthropology as an empirical science resting on anatomy and physiology, grounded in observation of intellectual and moral manifestations, in the study of the properties of the human race and of the manifestation of individual characteristics.

# Chapter: VI

**The character and meaning of Schopenhauer's pessimism – Schopenhauer's attitude to history – His political and social views – His indifference to national interests**

Not only among the broad public, but even among professional scholars, Schopenhauer is known chiefly as one of the principal representatives of the pessimistic tendency in philosophy. He is regarded as, as it were, its founder in modern philosophy. The number of followers of this tendency has been growing especially rapidly in recent times, and pessimistic philosophy became particularly widespread in Europe from the end of the 1860s, almost simultaneously with the publication of Eduard von Hartmann's *Philosophy of the Unconscious*, written in the spirit of Schopenhauer. Therefore, we consider it helpful to dwell in somewhat greater detail on the character and meaning of Schopenhauerian pessimism, which, if not the most striking and outstanding, is in any case the aspect of his teaching best known to the general public.

Many have asked about the causes, origin, and character of Schopenhauer's pessimistic world view, which showed itself in him already at a very young age. In this connection, it has been pointed out that he was born, raised, and lived under very satisfactory external conditions, that he was a fully secure man who could follow his inclinations without hindrance. The starting point of such perplexities is the strange assumption that in order to be an optimist or a pessimist one must be in happy or unhappy circumstances, or that pessimism is the result of disappointments and sorrows experienced in life. However, first, it is by no means proper that everyone who lives badly or has to live in sad times necessarily becomes a pessimist, and conversely that everyone to whom life smiles or who lives in a reasonable time becomes an optimist. True, with many people, optimism and pessimism do arise from purely subjective sources: they transfer their inner coloring onto external objects. If a person feels bright and cheerful in his soul, the whole world is bright and cheerful for him. If it is dark and sad in his soul, the whole world is sad and dark. Such people can be optimists today and pessimists tomorrow, and vice versa. However, such optimism and pessimism have no philosophical significance, since they are purely subjective. However, there exists another kind of optimism and pessimism, so to speak, of a philosophical character, whose cause has nothing in common either with subjective conditions or with the conditions of the time. It was precisely this kind of pessimism that Schopenhauer had.

Schopenhauer considers it one of the most significant errors of almost all metaphysical systems that they regard evil as something negative. On the contrary, it is something positive, something that makes itself felt. Evil, in his opinion, is inevitable as a consequence of affirming the will to live. There exists not only affirmation of the will to live, but also its denial, even its complete abolition. In this latter case, a completely different world, a completely different existence appears, of which we indeed have no conception and which seems to us nothing, yet not an absolute nothing, but only a relative one. Properly speaking, pessimism can be spoken of only when evil is considered incurable, and the one suffering from it irretrievably lost. Schopenhauer's pessimism is not of this sort. He considers deliverance from the world's evil possible, though only by way of a radical cure, a complete rebirth and renewal. Some find consolation against the mass of evil in the world in religion, others in art. Schopenhauer seeks and finds it in the growth of knowledge. "The only good side of life," Schopenhauer wrote back in 1814, "lies in the fact that alongside will there also exists knowing; this ensures will's ultimate deliverance." An ordinary pessimist, a pessimist from egoistic motives, a pessimist tired of life, would seek and find consolation in suicide. This consolation has indeed been resorted to from time immemorial by immoral pessimists for whom life became burdensome. Schopenhauer, however, this pessimist par excellence, rejects suicide in the most decisive manner, and on deeply moral grounds.

Some see proof of Schopenhauer's pessimism, in the generally accepted and not exclusively philosophical sense of the word, also in his doctrine of the immutability of character, by which he supposedly takes away from man hope of improvement. From this, a direct conclusion is drawn that his teaching is morally hopeless: that by declaring character uncorrectable, he thereby deprives the sinner who longs for correction of moral consolation, just as a physician who declares a disease incurable deprives the patient who longs for healing of physical consolation. However, to refute this, one may point to Schopenhauer's teaching on freedom of the will, where, of course, this freedom lies not in separate actions and manifestations of will, but in its essence, in its entire direction. Actions always correspond to empirical character and therefore inevitably bear its imprint. Therefore, if the empirical character is egoistic and accessible only to egoistic motives, then actions will inevitably be egoistic. However, character in general can be of another kind, since man is not bound for all eternity to his empirical character. As long as he is an egoist, he must inevitably act as an egoist, but he can cease to be an egoist, and then his actions will be guided not by egoistic but by moral motives. The immutability of character of which Schopenhauer speaks concerns only empirical character, not intellectual, non-material character (*intelligibler Charakter*). Thus, this immutability has only relative, not absolute significance. Therefore, there is hardly any basis for considering his doctrine of the immutability of character hopeless. Nor can hopelessness be seen in the fact that, according to this doctrine, moral good can be achieved only on the condition that the whole person becomes different. If so, one would have to consider Christianity hopeless and without consolation as well, since it too makes man's salvation depend on rebirth or renewal. To consider it hopeless would be to consider hopeless the words of a physician who promises a patient healing only on the condition that he changes his entire way of life and ceases to violate his nature.

Just as the philosopher Fichte was repeatedly reproached for not correctly understanding nature, Schopenhauer was reproached for not assigning history its proper place in the sphere of human knowledge. Indeed, the contempt with which he treats history belongs among the weakest points of his system, though on the other hand, it cannot be denied that it follows quite logically from his basic idea.

The essence of Schopenhauer's view of history, as outlined in *The World as Will and Representation*, is approximately as follows.

History is not a science, since it lacks the fundamental trait of science, the mutual causality of the phenomena it treats. Instead, it presents only correlation. Therefore, no system of history can exist, whereas systems exist for every other science. History is knowledge, not science, because nowhere does it arrive at knowledge of the particular by means of the general, but is forced to assimilate the particular directly and, so to speak, to grope its way in the realm of experience. In contrast, true sciences, having assimilated broader concepts, stand above particular facts. Sciences, as systems of concepts, always treat of kinds and classes, while history treats only of individuals. Sciences treat of what exists constantly, history only of what existed and ceased to exist. Moreover, since history has to deal only with what is personal and individual, which by its nature is endlessly diverse, it has only an incomplete, imperfect concept of everything. Finally, it must acquire ever-new data and knowledge with each day and each new fact, which deprives it of any character of completeness. History, always keeping in view only particular, individual facts and considering only facts as something exclusively real, is, in Schopenhauer's opinion, the direct opposite of philosophy, which looks at all that exists from the most general standpoint and has as its object only what is general, what remains identical even in the particular. While history teaches us that in each given time something new existed, philosophy seeks to convince us that at all times the same has been, is, and will be. In reality, the essence of human life, like the essence of nature, is everywhere and always fully present. Therefore, in order to understand it correctly, only a certain depth of conception is needed. History, however, hopes to replace depth with breadth and length. For it, the present is only some fragment that must be supplemented by the past, and whose length is infinite because it is lost in an infinite future. The difference between philosophers and historians, in Schopenhauer's view, is that the former wish to comprehend, while the latter wish to enumerate.

Schopenhauer maintains that history stands immeasurably lower not only than science and philosophy, but even than art. The content of art is the idea; the content of science is the concept.

Therefore, both art and science occupy themselves with what exists eternally and in the same way, and not with what now is but formerly was not and later will not be, what now exists thus but earlier existed otherwise and later will exist otherwise again. In other words, both art and philosophy deal with what Plato already saw as the object of actual knowledge. The content of history, on the contrary, is the particular, the fleeting linkings and interweavings of the shifting human race, upon which the most insignificant circumstances can influence. From this standpoint, the field of history can hardly be considered something worthy of serious study by the human mind. Fully agreeing with Aristotle that poetry is, so to speak, more philosophical than history, Schopenhauer assigns the former a far more important place than the latter. Poetry has done, and does, more for the knowledge of the essence of humanity than history.

True, both experience and history teach us to know man, or rather people, that is, they provide empirical information about the mutual relations of people. However, they do not allow us to look into the depths of man's inner essence. History relates to poetry as, for example, portrait painting relates to historical painting: the first conveys individual likeness, the second a more general likeness. The first has in view the truth of appearance, the second the truth of the idea – the poet deliberately and by choice places outstanding personalities in outstanding situations. The historian takes both as they come to hand. He has to view events not from the standpoint of their inner, true meaning that expresses an idea. However, from the standpoint of their external, apparent, relative meaning in connection with their consequences and complications, since his contemplation proceeds from the principle of cause, and in a given phenomenon, he sees only the external form of the latter. The poet, on the contrary, grasps ideas, the essence of humanity, outside any relation to time and circumstance.

From this standpoint, Schopenhauer even assigns greater importance than history to simple biographies, partly because the latter provide more precise and complete positive data than the former, and partly because in history, not so much separate people as peoples and armies play a prominent role. It is challenging, on a large scale of historical events, to trace the activity of individual persons. By contrast, a faithfully conveyed life of a single person depicts, within a narrower sphere, human activity in all its shades and forms. Moreover, in the sense of the inner significance of what happened, which alone matters, it is entirely indifferent whether events are small or significant, whether they occur in peasant huts or in royal palaces. In itself, all this has no significance and acquires it only through its relation to will. Just as a circle with a diameter of an inch and a circle with a diameter of forty million miles possess the same geometrical properties. Hence, the events and deeds of some village and of a vast state are in essence the same, and humanity can be studied and known in both.

To these two reasons for Schopenhauer's contemptuous attitude toward history, that it is not properly a science because it deals only with the particular, temporal, accidental, and that it gives far less for knowledge of the essence of humanity than art, poetry, and biography, a third is added, namely that history lacks unity, wholeness, and logical connection. He polemicizes energetically against attempts by post-Hegelian philosophy to present history as "something constructed according to a definite plan," to create from it an "organic whole." Since only the individual, and not the human race, possesses an absolute, immediate unity of consciousness, the unity of the course of life of the human race is a pure fiction. Moreover, just as in nature only the species is real and genus a mere abstraction, so in the human race only the individual and his life are honest, while peoples and their lives are something abstract. Only what happens within a person as a manifestation of his will is real, since only will can be considered something really existing, something *an und für sich* [in itself (Ger.)].

Schopenhauer sees the task of broadly and philosophically understood history as indicating the core that remains constantly the same and identical amid the varied, constantly changing shells. It is not history in itself that is devoid of significance, but a superficial, unreasonable understanding of its essence and its tasks that stops at the shell and does not strive to become more closely acquainted with the core. Without in any way diminishing the significance of history, Schopenhauer praises the ancient historians precisely because they depict particulars in such a way that "the ideal side of humanity expressed in them comes to the surface." The very preference Schopenhauer gives biographies over history becomes intelligible only insofar as these biographies meet the conditions he himself sets. And not only biographies, but epic and dramatic works become more coherent the more firmly they stand on historical ground. Purely invented characters and deeds are by no means capable of inspiring in us the same interest as historical ones that acquaint us with real destinies, with the real struggle of humanity. Therefore, all truly great poets draw material for their works from history. Tragedies, in Schopenhauer's view, satisfy in us not the sense of beauty but the sense of the sublime, and sublime characters and deeds we encounter chiefly in history.

History for the human race is the same as the intellect for an individual person. Thanks to the intellect, man gains the possibility of not being limited, like an animal, to a narrow, vivid present. However, he acquires the capacity to grasp a much broader past with which this present is connected and from which it arose, and also, based on the present and the past, to draw conclusions about the future. A people that does not know its own history is necessarily limited to acquaintance with the generation contemporary to it. Hence, it does not know itself and its present, since it cannot connect the latter with the past and explain the present by means of the past. Still less can it foresee the future. Only history gives a people full self-consciousness. Therefore, history should be viewed as the rational self-consciousness of the human race. For the latter, it is the same as the coherent self-consciousness conditioned by reason is for an individual, by the absence of which an animal is confined to the narrow realm of the tangible present. Therefore, every gap in history is a gap in the self-consciousness of humanity. Thus, history is the rational self-consciousness of the human race. It is the self-consciousness immediately inherent in the whole species, so that only through it does the latter truly become one whole, one humanity.

From these words of Schopenhauer it is clear that in his later works he somewhat diverged from himself regarding the role he assigned history in his earliest works, that he ceased to treat it with the former contempt and to see in it only a long, heavy, and obscure dream, and that finally he decided to assign history a more honorable place among the sciences, in the sphere of human knowledge.

Connected with Schopenhauer's views on history, its role and significance, are his views on the political and social orders of his time. From the study of history, he came to the conviction that only in sporadic cases does victory remain on the side of the just cause, that a just cause most often compromises itself and perishes from an excess of principle. Thus, for example, an excess of the monarchical principle produced a republic, and an excess of republican zeal led to the Terror of 1793 and to the cynicism of the Directory. He proceeds from the principle that the state is conceivable only under the condition of a double limitation of the will of the individual person, namely, limitation not only physical but also moral. The individual, imposing limitations on himself, does so for the sake of his own rationally understood interests. The state is not directed against egoism as such. On the contrary, it arises precisely from rationally understood egoism, methodically proceeding, rising from a one-sided viewpoint to a more general one, and resulting from the summation of a whole mass of individual egoisms. Therefore, the state is created not at all in order to counteract egoism, supposedly contrary to the principles of morality, but only in order to counteract the harmful consequences of the collision of many personal egoisms, which could harmfully affect the well-being of individuals.

However, the matter does not end with this first limitation of personal egoism or arbitrariness. One must inevitably take into account the intellectual imperfection and moral weakness of the individuals that make up the state, which necessitates further limitation of the will of the individual and thereby a further deviation from a purely ethical direction. The first limitation lay in the subordination of all to one common rule, the law, and could be considered morally expedient. The second limitation is carried out at the expense of abstract right, since state power, in order for the state to exist, must rest not only on force but even partly on untruth.

Thus, in Schopenhauer's opinion, a state governed by right is nothing other than a fiction.

Politics, the more clearly it understands its task, the sooner it becomes a science that has in view first of all immediate needs. As for the principle of power itself, Schopenhauer, on the one hand, denies any mortal the right to rule a people against that people's will. However, on the other hand, he calls those same people "an eternally minor sovereign," who must constantly remain under guardianship and to whom the right to govern itself cannot be granted without exposing it to the most significant dangers, since it, like all minors, easily becomes a toy in the hands of clever rogues called demagogues. A right that I am not able to use, I do not, in fact, possess. Therefore, Schopenhauer reduces all state power to its establishment by a law of nature, and, in agreement with all true philosophers from Aristotle to Schleiermacher, preaches a state bond not ethical but purely physical. He considers republics something "unnatural, artificially created, begotten by reflection." Therefore, he justifies the monarchical principle, while not denying a representative system. He wittily remarks that right is chemically analogous to alcohol, prussic acid, fluorine, and so forth, which are never found in a pure and isolated state but only in certain compounds that give them the necessary density. Therefore, right, in order to be able to exist and act in our real and material world with its ideal, ethereal properties, it inevitably needs an admixture of arbitrariness and violence, without which it would evaporate without residue.

The arbitrary, artificially created classification of plants devised by Linnaeus cannot be replaced by any natural classification, however rational the latter may be, since it would lack that firmness and clarity of definitions inherent in an artificial classification. In the same way, an artificial and arbitrary basis of state structure cannot be replaced by a purely natural basis. The correctness of this view is demonstrated, in Schopenhauer's opinion, by the unsuccessful attempts of the South American republics to create their state structure on the principle of abstract right: there go hand in hand the basest utilitarianism, coarseness, all kinds of political trickery, outrageous slavery, repudiation of debts, robbery, and ever increasing ochlocracy, on the one hand, and the loudest political phrases and the most perfected forms of supposedly political freedom, on the other.

"Everywhere and at all times," says Schopenhauer, "there existed strong dissatisfaction with governments, laws, and social institutions, but this happened mostly because people are always ready to shift onto governments, laws, and institutions the responsibility for the evil inseparable from human existence, listening to certain eloquent demagogues. The world in itself, by its structure, is wonderful, created for universal happiness and well-being. Everything bad found in this best of worlds they attribute to governments. If governments did what they should do, then there would be the kingdom of heaven on earth, that is, all people could, without any labor or effort, eat, drink, multiply, and die as much as they pleased."

Although Schopenhauer's political convictions were rooted in recognition of the necessity of a decisive predominance of the principle of authority in the state, and although he insistently demanded "respect for monarchs," since their very existence is beneficial because they are, in his conviction, a defense against ochlocracy and anarchy, it by no means follows that he was an advocate of despotism. Regarding events in Italy in the last years of his life, he said that legitimacy does not yet confer a right to success. In order to secure success, a government must stand intellectually above the masses it governs. In moral terms, it must not be too noble, like Titus, but on the other hand, it must not stand below the generally widespread legal consciousness either.

Schopenhauer was utterly foreign to national vanity. He even stated that all his patriotism was reduced to using the German language. He did not even like being considered a German and did not miss an opportunity to point to his Dutch origin. For this energetic man, the boastfulness and imitativeness of German politics were so repugnant that he mercilessly condemned in Germans precisely what he left unnoticed or even excused in other people. For the breadth of a philosopher's view, this absolute absence of narrow German patriotism was even advantageous. He never touched on particular political questions, still less local ones. He stood above them and related to major political events with Olympian grandeur. Only when they came too close to him and threatened to disturb his intellectual and spiritual peace did he begin to be agitated. During the September days of 1848, his fear of the onset of ochlocracy reached the highest degree, and he seriously considered fleeing Frankfurt. However, in calmer times, he found that journalists went much farther than he did in their pessimism, though this was done mostly not from conviction but for personal gain. He liked to repeat that in political matters, people, least of all, know what is beneficial and what is harmful for them, and whether a given event will serve their benefit or their harm.

# Chapter: VII

**Views on women and on love – Manner of creation – The paradoxical character of Schopenhauer**

Schopenhauer, by his convictions, was not only a misanthrope, though only in a conditional sense, as we explained above, but also a misogynist (a hater of women) and a misogamist (a hater of marriage). He maintained that nature itself had shortchanged women in the spiritual and rational respects. She is distinguished by intellectual short-sightedness, is inclined to take the appearance of things for the essence of the matter, and to prefer trifles to serious business. The mental gaze of a woman, being preeminently immediate, is able to distinguish objects that are nearby, but is incapable of going beyond a limited horizon. Everything past, distant, and absent makes only a weak impression on a woman. Owing to this same inborn near-sightedness, a woman is inclined to wastefulness. On the other hand, precisely because a woman gives herself to the present more than a man does and is more capable than he is of enjoying a more or less tolerable life, she possesses greater cheerfulness and clarity of spirit. Moreover, perceiving things differently from men and always marking out the shortest path to a goal, a woman is distinguished by greater sobriety of views than a man and sees in things only what they actually contain.

Thus, precisely owing to the weakness of the female intellect, everything visible, immediate, and real has far greater power over women than abstract ideas do. Therefore, a woman yields more easily to feelings of compassion and sympathy, but in matters of justice, fairness, and conscientiousness, she yields to man. As a weaker creature, a woman finds an instrument of self-defense in cunning. "She," says Schopenhauer, "is instinctively sly, yet at the same time, through unreason and poor wit, absurd, capricious, vain, greedy for glitter, pomp, and tinsel. In their relations with one another, women display greater constraint, secrecy, and hostility than men do in their relations among themselves. Women lack a true vocation for music, poetry, and art in general. Even the most brilliant representatives of the female sex never created anything truly great and original in the artistic sphere. Still less are they capable of astonishing the world with a learned work of enduring merit. This is explained by the fact that a woman is always and in everything doomed only to a mediocre dominion through the man whom alone she possesses directly. Women in all respects are the second sex, weak, standing below men. By their very nature, women are undoubtedly doomed to obedience. This is already evident from the fact that any one of them, once she comes into an independent position, voluntarily gives herself into the guardianship of a lover or a confessor, if only some man might rule over her."

With such a view of women, Schopenhauer's skepticism regarding the feeling of love becomes understandable, a skepticism that at times approaches cynicism. In his opinion, love, however Platonic it may seem, everywhere and always has been, is, and will be nothing other than a more definite and strictly individualized sexual striving whose ultimate unconscious aim is the birth of a future human being. In this sense, love as sexual impulse is "the will to life in itself." A person, feeling love and attraction to a woman, in essence, only obeys an instinct directed to the benefit and advantage of the species. The true aim of any earthly romance is the bringing forth of a new individual. Of course, love has many gradations. The more passionate the lover, the more the beloved person, by her qualities, satisfies the needs and requirements of the lover. However, that love, in essence, is nothing other than an instinct directed to the preservation of the type of the species and to its strongest possible multiplication, is evident from the motives by which an individual is guided in choosing the object of passion. These motives, according to Schopenhauer, are of three kinds: motives that contribute to preserving the type of the species in the physical respect; motives that have in view the maintenance of the spiritual traits of the species; and finally motives that aim at correcting the defects of both begetters.

By the circumstance that, in Schopenhauer's view, love is grounded in instincts directed exclusively to the good of the species, he also explains why the very feeling that binds lovers proves short-lived. From the moment love is satisfied, the man begins to cool toward the object of his attraction. "Thus," says Schopenhauer, "the good of the whole species is the object of love. Compared with this task, personal strivings are insignificant. The genius of the species willingly sacrifices all individual interests, unswervingly pursuing its chief and only aim, the maintenance of the species, amid the turmoil of war and the disorders of civil life, in time of plague, and in the quiet of monasteries." This leads Schopenhauer to consider the question of monogamy and polygamy, and he most decisively, again in the interests of the species, inclines in favor of polygamy, or rather tetrogamy, that is, fourfold marriage.

Expressing his views on marriage, bigamy, and polygamy, partly paradoxical and partly even diverging from generally accepted notions of morality, Schopenhauer nevertheless shows a decisive preference for celibacy. As if for the future shame of those who reproached his teaching with immorality, he presents voluntary virginity as the only means of liberation from a world of sinfulness and calamities. Turning to the question of where, sooner, in married life or in celibacy, that untroubled existence can be achieved which is necessary for people of intellectual labor, for scholars, Schopenhauer readily referred to Descartes, Malebranche, Spinoza, Leibniz, and Kant, who remained bachelors all their lives. He also liked to repeat, together with Petrarch: "He who seeks peace must avoid women, that eternal source of disputes and storms." He believed that a thinker, by the rational character of his nature, is little accessible to the joys and pleasures of the domestic hearth and that he risks, because of insignificant and indifferent trifles from his point of view, sacrificing his independence, seclusion, and peaceful intellectual self-enjoyments.

By his character, Schopenhauer did not belong to the number of rational people, those calm, even characters who live chiefly by concepts. He should instead be assigned to the category of people who are lively, impulsive, influenced by the present, living chiefly by their personal views, whether these pertain to reality or to fantasy. Here, a question naturally arises: is such a character suitable for a philosopher? Should a philosopher not be the coolest-headed being in the world? People do speak of those who keep their composure where others grow heated: that is a philosopher. To this, Lindner explains that if one looks at the matter from the generally accepted notion connected with the word "philosophy," then only a cold, rational person, who cannot be vigorously shaken or thrown off balance, is capable of it. However, it was precisely this view that Schopenhauer considered wrong and superficial in his opinion; philosophy issues from the same source as art. It is essentially art, thinking in words, that is, in concepts. In other words, the activity of reason has the same significance as technique in art. For the thinker, abstract concepts are what canvas and paints are for a painter. "Philosophy," he says, "is far from being an algebraic problem, and Vauvenargues is absolutely right in asserting that great thoughts come from the heart." If one accepts such a standpoint as correct, then the objection that Schopenhauer could not be a good thinker simply because he lacked cool-headedness falls away. If philosophy is an art, then cool-headedness is necessary only when what has been seen and deeply felt must be depicted in a vivid form. However, to see and to feel, one need not be cool-headed. This applies equally to the poet and to the thinker.

Just as a poet must live through the impulses and states he depicts, or at least deeply sympathize with those who lived through them, so the thinker must, in general, experience in himself the essence of that life whose picture he presents to us. He must, so to speak, enlarge his soul to the dimensions of the world soul. For both poet and thinker, cool-headedness is needed only when what has been lived and felt within must be presented objectively, as something of universal significance. Furthermore, such cool-headedness, necessary for depicting what has been lived and felt, Schopenhauer possessed in the highest degree. He possessed it in philosophy in the same measure as Goethe and Shakespeare possessed it in poetry. This explains the objectivity with which he depicts the world as will, and the living truth of that depiction. In the same sense in which it was said of Goethe that he was a poet "on occasion," one may also say of Schopenhauer that he was a thinker "on occasion." His philosophical propositions were primarily written in connection with something he had lived through and experienced, and only then were systematized. This is proved, among other things, by the very form of his manuscripts, consisting predominantly of aphorisms. Therefore, with regard to Schopenhauer more than to any other thinker, one can, based on his works, form a conclusion about his personality.

This manner of creating also explains that intellectual labor was for him by no means as straightforward a matter as one might conclude from his style. Seeing how easily and clearly he expresses the most profound thoughts, one might conclude that he needed only to write down what his genius dictated to him. However, although thinking was for Schopenhauer as easy as, for example, walking, and although the course of his thoughts was as swift and elastic as his physical gait, it would be mistaken to conclude from this that thoughts were born ready-made in his head and that he did not have to think, and think much, think strenuously. On this matter, he himself expressed himself as follows: "The eye becomes dulled from long looking at the same object and ends by ceasing to distinguish objects. So too the mind, through prolonged reflection on the same subject, becomes dulled and ceases to grasp that subject's distinctive properties. Then one must drop the matter in order to return to it later with fresh forces. In the brain, too, there are, as it were, tides and ebbs."

In one of his letters written in 1813, when he was only twenty-five, he wrote as follows:

"When some thought arises in my brain in an unclear form and is drawn before me in misty outlines, an irresistible desire seizes me to grasp it. I drop everything and pursue that thought like a hunter his game through all the windings, try to cut it off, until I seize it, overcome it, and set it down on paper. However, sometimes it happens that the thought still slips away from me. Then I must patiently wait until some other occasion again stirs it from its place. If during such a chase after a thought some external noise interferes with me, I experience a purely physical suffering." This largely explains Schopenhauer's sensitivity to any noise and his desire to establish around himself as far as possible an ideal silence. Both in *The World as Will and Representation* and in his *Parerga*, he devoted special chapters to the question "On Noise."

Apart from the effort Schopenhauer's mental work cost him, especially amid external noise, this work proceeded in his brain with a kind of natural inevitability. He himself said that he always worked and wrote as if obeying some unconscious instinct. "A guarantee of the correctness, and therefore the solidity, of my philosophy," he wrote in 1824, "for me lies in the fact that I did not create it at all, but that it created itself. My philosophical propositions arose in me without any participation on my part, in moments when every willing in me seemed to fall asleep, and reason, without any deliberate direction this way or that, seized impressions of the real world and made them run parallel with thinking, again without any participation of my will. However, together with will every individualization disappear. Therefore, my personality had nothing to do with it. Here, contemplation took shape in concepts, pure objective contemplation, or, in other words, the objective world itself chose my head as its arena, since it found it suitable for this purpose.

Furthermore, what does not issue from the individual cannot be the possession of one individual. It belongs only to reason and is identical, by its character though not by degree, in all individuals. Therefore, in time, all individuals must converge upon it. I merely, as a spectator and eyewitness, wrote down what at such moments appeared to me as an understanding alien to any participation of will, and then used what was written down for my works. This serves as the guarantee of their truth, and this consciousness will not allow me to stray from the path, however long my works may remain unrecognized" (1824).

Schopenhauer himself, with such a view of intellectual work, without any false modesty, had a very high opinion of his own mind. "The measure of my mind," he wrote, "may be seen in those cases in which, in explaining wholly special phenomena, I competed with outstanding men: with Newton and Goethe in the theory of colors, with Winckelmann, Lessing, and Goethe in the interpretation of the statue of Laocoön, with Kant and Jean Paul in the explanation of the comic." On the other hand, being of high opinion of his mind, Schopenhauer at the same time acknowledged that mind and intellect in general, as something physical, as the brain activity of an organic body, can flourish only for a comparatively short time, and that having reached its culminating point, it declines. This consciousness Schopenhauer applied to his own mind as well. When he reached thirty-eight, he considered his intellect already on the wane. "At the time," he wrote in 1826, "when my mind stood at its culminating point, when under favorable circumstances my brain was able to attain the highest degree of tension, then whatever object my gaze fell upon, I was dealing with revelations and in my head there appeared a whole series of thoughts worthy of being written down, and therefore written down. Now, however, when I have turned thirty-eight, when I am growing old, when heavenly inspiration is declining, it may happen that I will stand before Raphael's Madonna and it will say nothing to me." In general, Schopenhauer assigned the flourishing of the male mind the same duration as the flourishing of female beauty, that is, about fifteen years, from the age of twenty to thirty-five. "The twenties and the first half of the thirties," he wrote, "are for the human intellect what the month of May is for trees, which only then bloom and set fruit." Indeed, if one compares Schopenhauer's works of old age, which he himself titled *Senilia*, with his earlier works, one cannot avoid the conclusion that he was to a certain extent right and that the general law of nature made itself felt in his mind as well. In general, Schopenhauer's most original, basic views should be sought in his earlier works, whereas the later ones represent only a further development and confirmation of those views.

One thing runs like a red thread through all his works, both early and later: the paradoxical character of his world view. He himself was aware of this paradoxical character, but he not only did not consider it a defect, but he saw in it a favorable sign. Thus, for example, he wrote in 1815: "If someone is prejudiced against the paradoxical character of some work, this obviously happens from the conviction that there is already a sufficient quantity of truth in circulation, that humanity in general has already achieved much, and that it remains only to correct and supplement particulars. However, he who, like Plato and Goethe, is convinced that the world is full of absurdities will always see in the paradoxical character of a work a favorable symptom, though not a decisive one. The world, of course, would be beautiful if truth in it did not have to be paradoxical, if virtue in it did not have to suffer, if everything beautiful deserved universal approval. However, where can one find such a world?" In that same year 1815 he wrote: "He who has written a great, immortal work, the reception given to that work by the public and the judgments of critics about it are as little capable of grieving or disturbing him as, for example, the abuse and insults of the insane are capable of offending a mentally healthy person walking through a madhouse, assuming of course that this person has a proper understanding of where exactly he is." One should note, however, that Schopenhauer, being very sensitive to the attacks of his learned opponents, himself somewhat diverged from the views he expressed theoretically in the words cited above.

# Sources

1. Wilhelm Gwinner. *Arthur Schopenhauer, aus persönlichem Umgange dargestellt. Ein Blick auf sein Leben, seinen Charakter und seine Lehre.* Leipzig, 1862.

2. Ernst Otto Lindner. *Arthur Schopenhauer. Von ihm. Über ihn. Ein Wort der Vertheidigung und Memorabilien, Briefe und Nachlassstücke von Julius Frauenstädt.* Berlin, 1863.

3. Otto Busch. *Arthur Schopenhauer.* Munich, 1878.

4. Julius Frauenstädt. *Neue Briefe über die Schopenhauer'sche Philosophie.* Leipzig, 1876.

5. Foucher-de-Careil. *Hegel et Schopenhauer. Études sur la philosophie allemande moderne, depuis Kant jusque'à nos jours.* Paris, 1862.

6. Th. Ribot. *La Philosophie de Schopenhauer (Bibliothèque de Philosophie contemporaine).* Paris, 1888.

7. Rudolph Seydel. *Schopenhauer's philosophisches System (Gekrönte Preisschrift).* Leipzig, 1857.

8. V. Stein. *Schopenhauer as a Man and Thinker (1788–1860). An Attempt at a Biography.* Vol. 1. St. Petersburg, 1887.

9. *Proceedings of the Moscow Psychological Society.* Issue I. 1888. "Arthur Schopenhauer: Essays on His Life and Teaching (On the Occasion of the Centenary of His Birth)." Articles: V. I. Stein, "Biographical Sketch"; N. Ya. Grot, "On the Significance of Schopenhauer's Philosophy"; L. M. Lopatin, "Schopenhauer's Moral Teaching"; V. P. Preobrazhensky, "Essay on Schopenhauer's Theory of Knowledge."

Printed in Dunstable, United Kingdom